THE NEW JOB CONTRACT

THE NEW JOB CONTRACT

ECONOMIC JUSTICE IN AN AGE OF INSECURITY

BARBARA HILKERT ANDOLSEN

The Pilgrim Press
Cleveland, Ohio

IN MEMORY OF

Wayne D. and Helen Bennett McMurray,

whose generosity

made this work possible

The Pilgrim Press, Cleveland, Ohio 44115
Copyright © 1998 by Barbara Hilkert Andolsen

Biblical quotations are from the New Revised Standard Version of the Bible, © 1989 by the Division of Christian Education of the National Council of the Churches of Christ in the U.S.A., and are used by permission

Published 1998. All rights reserved

Printed in the United States of America on acid-free paper

03 02 01 00 99 98   5 4 3 2 1

Library of Congress Cataloging-in-Publication Data
Andolsen, Barbara Hilkert.
    The new job contract : economic justice in an age of insecurity /
Barbara Hilkert Andolsen.
        p.   cm.
    Includes bibliographical references (p.   ) and index.
    ISBN 0-8298-1272-5 (pbk. : alk. paper)
    1. Economics—Religious aspects—Christianity.   2. Job security—
Moral and ethical aspects.   I. Title.
BR115.E3A53   1998
261.8'5—dc21
                                                        98-35073
                                                        CIP

CONTENTS

PREFACE

The terms of the social contract between employers and employees in the United States have changed. Employers are no longer held accountable for providing employment security for workers. The responsibility for creating economic security for workers and their dependents is being shifted squarely onto the workers themselves. As an ethicist, I consider economic security an important human good. I am disturbed by a situation in which it seems that many people in the working and middle classes are facing a loss of economic security. Others who are poor, including the working poor, are being pushed even further away from positions of economic security. I have written this book because I believe that it is important for ethicists to examine what is, in the business press, being termed "employability."

The transition to a social paradigm of "employability"—a model that explicitly excludes a promise of employment security but does offer workers a chance to develop skills that will make them "employable" in the external labor market—has probably been taking place for more than two decades. However, the shift has come into clearer focus during the 1990s. First, during the recession of 1990–91, an unprecedented number of professionals and middle managers (most of them white) lost their jobs. When job loss hit middle-class white-collar workers, mainstream media such as *The New York Times, Business Week,* and *Fortune* told the American public that something unprecedented was happening.

Unemployment and economic insecurity among poor persons of color were an old story, but economic anxiety among the white upper-middle class was something new.

Second, in a drive for consistent double-digit rates of return for their stockholders, major corporations have been slashing employment throughout the economic "recovery" Americans have been "enjoying" for the last seven years. These developments have made it plain that many workers in the United States can no longer rely on their employers to provide them with economic security. As a religious ethicist, I urge religious groups to ask, Is the employability contract fair to workers? Is the employability model consistent with life together in a good society? Religious groups ought to support national and international efforts to promote economic security for workers and their loved ones under changing labor market conditions.

Throughout my scholarly career, I have focused on feminist religious ethics. I came to the current study through earlier work on contingent employment. Women are the majority of contingent workers. As I will discuss in this book, gender assumptions about women as family caregivers intersect with contingent work arrangements in ways that are potentially detrimental to women. I started the research for this book concerned about growing economic insecurity for women. As I learned more about job tenure as a key indicator of employment security, I came to see a more complex pattern in which some women were making economic gains while some men, including some older male professionals and managers, were suffering serious economic losses. Prodded by womanist ethicists, I had already recognized that many men of color suffered forms of oppression that challenged any simplistic moral analysis that described injustice only along the axis of gender. In working on this book, what I learned about the economic perils facing many white men—primarily, but not exclusively, men with limited education or job training—has made my social analysis even more complicated. There are places in this book where the well-being of women is not a sufficiently comprehensive moral norm.

In addition, while working on this book, I have examined economic data that shows that a significant minority of wage-earning women are now in well-paying long-term professional and managerial jobs. While I acknowledge that some women have made significant economic gains, I in no way want to obscure the reality of pervasive gender discrimination in the workplace. Women as a group have not achieved economic parity with their male peers. Nevertheless, the substantial economic progress made by some women raises, for me, sharp questions about the moral responsibilities of economically "successful" women. What are the possibilities of a solidarity that will bind those privileged women to the women and men who are excluded or marginalized in the labor markets of the information age? Thus, while gender remains a key analytic category for me, my work here does not fit comfortably within the boundaries of what I have previously understood as feminist ethics.

Still, gender equality remains a central moral value in this book. My commitment to the equality of women and men makes the language used to name the Divine Being a difficult problem for me. Many traditional Christian names for the Deity have masculine connotations. Throughout much of Christian history, Christians lived in patriarchal societies, where it seemed uniquely appropriate to use images of socially superior males as metaphors for the Supreme Being. Now, however, in a time of profound social transformation in the relationships between women and men, those who continue to use overwhelmingly male language to describe the Deity are (sometimes inadvertently) bolstering male domination. I consider it a moral imperative not to reinscribe male supremacy through the words I use to denote the Divine Being.

Therefore, in this book I have used the following linguistic strategies. I have retained the exact language of direct quotes, of course. When I am presenting the position of thinkers who were comfortable with traditional masculine language for the Divine, I have sometimes used the word "God." In the rest of the text, I have used gender-neutral language for the Divine Being as much as possible. However, there is one classic Christian phrase I find very useful that is difficult to render in gender-neutral terms—the reign of God. In this case, I have substituted "God/dess" for "God." I intend the term "God/dess" used in this context to remind me and my readers that the Divine Being is *neither* male nor female. God/dess is beyond gender. Still, both male and female human beings are created in the image of God/dess, so it is appropriate to use a term that incorporates both male and female for the Divine Being, who is beyond male and female.

I have written this book particularly for readers interested in the application of Christian ethics to questions of economic justice, especially the question of the moral legitimacy of the new employability contract. In particular, I hope this book will help those ministering to parishes (whether as clergy or laity) to understand some of the important challenges that their parishioners are facing in the economic realm. I would like to help those engaged in pastoral activity to make connections among Christian values, Christian spirituality, and the experiences of Christian laity within a prosperous but turbulent United States economy. I hope that Christian believers who are striving to gain economic security for themselves and their loved ones under the new, and often more difficult, terms of the employability contract will find that this book sheds light on connections between their faith and their work lives.

While this book has been written primarily for a Christian audience, I welcome readers from other religious traditions and readers who do not consider themselves religious persons. This book draws upon Christian values and Christian ritual experience. However, I expect that readers from other religious faiths, particularly those of Jewish or Islamic background, will find that the basic ethical insights here resonate with values and practices in their own traditions. In addition, other readers, although not religious people themselves, will be interested in the issues of business ethics that are raised by the shift to a new social contract. They may wish to concentrate on the first through the third chapters and the relevant sections of the fourth and fifth chapters.

ACKNOWLEDGMENTS

I would like to thank people who supported me while I was pursuing this project. I am grateful for the ongoing support that the McMurray-Bennett Foundation gave me while I explored these questions.

A sabbatical leave from Monmouth University gave me a chance to do essential research. Colleagues at Monmouth provided crucial encouragement. They include Thomas Pearson, Kenneth Stunkel, Margaret DelGuercio, Brian Garvey, Ellen Mutari, Brian Greenberg, Susan Goulding, and James Stam.

I would also like to thank Timothy Sedgwick, Anne Patrick, Susan Ross, Elisabeth Johnson, Warren Copeland, Carol Robb, and the members of the Northeast Feminist Scholars for help and encouragement.

Librarians at Monmouth University, Drew University, Union Theological Seminary (New York), and the Research Centers of the New York Public Library assisted me with professionalism and courtesy.

Timothy Staveteig and the staff of Pilgrim Press shared my belief that questions of economic justice are important.

My daughter, Ruth, spent her last two years of high school in a home with a mother who was gestating a book and endured the experience with humor and love. My husband, Alan, shared his knowledge of the corporate world and provided extensive editorial and computer support.

I am very grateful to them all.

Today, Americans find themselves in the midst of a paradoxical prosperity. Jobs appear plentiful and the economy is growing, yet many families have less economic security. Other people who lack the skills necessary in a global, information economy face worsening economic marginalization.

In the spring of 1998, the United States economy is strong. The United States is experiencing the seventh year of sustained economic expansion. Unemployment has been below 5 percent for a year; unemployment rates are the lowest that they have been in a quarter century. (The unemployment rate for whites is 3.9 percent; however, for Hispanic Americans, it is 6.8 percent; and for blacks, it is 9.7 percent.)[1] The United States has been creating an enormous number of new jobs, and some economists say that many of those new jobs are in traditionally higher-paying managerial and professional fields. For the moment, the outlook seems good. However, there has been a disturbing underlying change in the employment relationship between many workers and their employers. This "new job contract" shifts more economic responsibility to workers and significantly transforms the basis for economic security for most individuals and families.

Throughout most of the 1990s, many individuals and families have been anxious about the future of their jobs. Americans find that the basic social understanding about the duration of a "good" job has changed. For decades after World War II, American society expected that good employers would normally offer long-term employment to workers who worked hard and performed their job duties adequately. However, beginning in the 1980s, major corporations that had offered employment security to workers began to "downsize"—firing many longtime employees. In addition, during the recession of 1990–91, an unusually high proportion of white-collar workers lost their jobs. In this decade, the largest American corporations have even slashed a number of middle-management jobs. When job losses cut into the security of white, middle-class, white-collar workers, the larger society realized that the terms of the implicit social contract concerning jobs had changed.

American workers are being offered a new deal—the employability contract. Under the employability contract at its best, the employer offers a job with good wages and decent fringe benefits. Importantly, the employer promises the employee challenging work assignments and, where necessary, training opportunities that will allow the employee to maintain top job skills. The employer does not—many say cannot—honestly promise long-term employment. The employer acknowledges openly that the employee has a job only as long as the employee's work promotes the company's immediate goals and enhances the company's short-term profitability. Still, the employer does promise to cooperate with the employee to enhance the employee's knowledge and skills. So, if the current employer decides to eliminate the employee's job, the employee should be able to find another good job quickly in the external labor market.

Many companies are also making extensive use of other forms of labor arrangements that involve even less organizational commitment to those doing the company's work. Corporations are hiring a significant number of contingent workers. There is a long-term trend toward the use of more part-timers, temporary workers, and contract workers. While some people welcome the flexibility that contingent work can provide, the majority of contingent workers would prefer to have full-time jobs that offer standard wages and benefits and continuing employment. In this book, I examine a number of the serious disadvantages that accompany contingent work, such as a lack of health care or pension coverage, limited access to skills training at employer expense, or low probability of union representation. Particularly worrisome is the limited evidence that suggests that some workers are trapped in a situation of "permanent temporariness"—relying on a series of short-term jobs, perhaps interspersed with periods when they must depend on welfare benefits.

The shift to the employability paradigm and a greater use of contingent workers are limiting the economic security of many workers and their families. By economic security, I mean a well-founded confidence that one will be able to maintain one's material lifestyle and meet one's financial obligations now and in the future. I contend that economic security—minimally, security at a level consistent with dignified life in one's local community—is an important human good. In the United States, where government benefits (either through unemployment insurance, public assistance programs, or even social security) are relatively modest, most people must depend on the wages from their jobs, personal savings or investments (if any), and pension income for economic support during their working lives and throughout their retirement years. Since most Americans are heavily dependent on their own wages or those of family members, economic security is closely tied to an unbroken employment history. For most American families, a protracted period of unemployment for a major wage earner in the family badly erodes the family's economic well-being.

In this book, I will use the term "employment security" to describe a situation in which persons have reasonable confidence that they will remain employed, should they so desire, throughout the span of a normal work life. (I do recognize that some workers will voluntarily elect to take some breaks in employment in order to fulfill other goals such as full-time education or caring for dependent family members or loved ones.) Some writers call confidence about continuing employment "job security." However, "job security" can be an ambiguous term. It is used by some persons to mean what I have just described as employment security. Other writers use "job security" to mean a well-founded confidence that one will remain employed in one's present job with the same basic duties well into the future. In a dynamic economy, I believe that job security in this latter, more narrow sense is an unreasonable social goal. As both technology and the economy change, some jobs become obsolete. Seeking job security for workers in such jobs can result in more harm than good. For example, in some cases where powerful unions have insisted on job security in a narrow sense for their workers, the results have been highly destructive to jobs after only a few years. One vivid case was the insistence of the longshoremen's union in New York City that their members continue to unload ships manually, rather than use an innovative, labor-saving containerized shipping method. The nearby port in Elizabeth, New Jersey, did offer facilities for containerized shipping. Shippers diverted cargoes to the cheaper and more efficient operation in Elizabeth, and the piers of New York City became a wasteland. The union achieved job security for members with seniority at the cost of employment opportunities on the docks in New York for future workers.

I am concerned with employment security, not job security as it is narrowly understood. Proponents claim that the new employability contract and the use of contingent labor can be consistent with employment security for American workers. I am skeptical that they are correct. I am particularly concerned that the employability contract is not workable for employees with routine skills and for older employees. I am disturbed that contingent work continues a pattern of insecure work for many persons of color and for some white women. Those working as contingent workers or under the "employability" paradigm have diminished access to employment security as a human good.

When I began this project, I approached changing employment patterns as a feminist scholar, committed to exploring the impact of these economic changes on diverse groups of women. What I discovered about employment patterns challenged me to create a more complex analysis. Reviewing the data, I found distressing gaps among women from different racial and ethnic groups. In particular, I found that there had been a period in the 1960s and 1970s when the economic gaps between white and black women had narrowed as more black women moved from domestic and agricultural work into better-paying clerical positions. By the 1980s, however, younger white women were beginning to move into managerial and professional positions in greater numbers. Few black women were able to get such relatively high-paying jobs until quite recently. So, the economic gap between white and black women increased again. The disparity between women in the best-paying jobs and the worst-paying jobs has also been increasing, as women with a college education or better participate in the high rewards being reaped by better-educated workers in an information economy. The fortunes of women are polarizing sharply along class lines.

Even more challenging for a feminist ethicist, I found that many men, including many white men, are losing ground in this economy, while some economically privileged (primarily white) women are doing much better. For example, some men have been losing long-term jobs, while many women are spending more years with the same employer. These patterns of job duration are important because workers with long job tenure often make better wages and receive important rewards such as better pensions. Men with a limited education are suffering the greatest economic losses under current economic conditions. In addition, corporate downsizing has created a new set of economic "losers"—men over fifty-four. Men who lose a long-time position when they are older than fifty are finding it very hard to find comparable jobs with new employers. Such economic changes are raising new questions about the virtue of solidarity across lines of economic difference.

A central question for this book is, How can we morally evaluate these new employment patterns? I will present two sets of ethical resources for assessing the new job contract. The first is social contract thought as it has been applied to the field of business ethics. The social contract approach developed by Thomas Donaldson and Thomas Dunfee explores two types of social contracts, both relevant to evaluating the new job contract. Donaldson and Dunfee recognize that various social groups have implicit sets of moral expectations about corporate conduct. They call these social understandings extant social contracts, or microsocial contracts. Since the beliefs of social groups can be distorted by ignorance, excessive self-interest, or bigotry, extant social contracts require moral scrutiny. One technique for examining microsocial contracts is to perform a thought experiment that is designed to promote fairness. Donaldson offers us a thought experiment in which we imagine an original situation in which there were no joint economic ventures. He invites us to consider what moral obligations a group of reasonable persons would place on businesses before they allowed business entities to come into existence. Among other things, Donaldson insists that the social group would require that businesses make the economic prospects of workers better than their prospects would be as individual producers. Donaldson and Dunfee's work allows us to ask important questions about the new "employability" contract. Does this new employment relationship make the lives of workers better in ways that legitimate social support for those corporations that are offering jobs on "employability" terms?

Catholic social teachings offer other important insights. The Catholic social tradition has offered from its inception a more explicit critique of power relations rooted in economic disparities. Beginning with *Rerum Novarum,* the Catholic tradition has acknowledged the power that enables those who control the means of production to exploit the economic vulnerabilities of wage laborers. The Catholic tradition has been willing to call for strong moral constraints on financial capital, insisting that capital must be used in ways that create a widespread prosperity and promote the common good. Catholic social ethicists have begun to appreciate that many individuals increasingly achieve economic security through their possession of technical, professional, or managerial skills. They also recognize the precarious future for persons, in both developing and developed nations, who lack the skills to compete effectively in the labor markets of a global, information economy. This last concern is an example of an important moral stance that has figured prominently in Catholic social thought since the late 1960s—the fundamental option for the poor. In a situation of paradoxical prosperity, Catholic social teachings give special attention to those who are deprived of basic material goods and of economic security.

Still, both social contract theory and official Catholic social thought fail to give adequate attention to gender when addressing the situation of workers. Both forms of thought might accept, without sufficient critical scrutiny, contingent employment relationships *for women.* They might be too quick to accept an interpretation of contingent work for women that characterizes such work as a positive form of flexibility for both employer and employee. An explicit commitment to gender equality is necessary in order to draw attention to the many drawbacks that contingent work presents for female workers.

The new employability contract shifts the responsibility for economic security onto the individual. Current economic developments are pushing individuals apart, prodding them to pursue their own interests while weakening ties among workers, to the corporation, and among persons in society. Yet, moral life requires that we assume responsibility for the well-being of others and for the common good.

What resources are available to encourage solidarity in a period when economic security is diminished for many despite general prosperity?

For Christians, a eucharist-centered spirituality can provide a foundation for concern for the economic well-being of others, particularly for those who are the most vulnerable economically. Still, a consideration of the connections between the eucharist and ethics is difficult for me because our celebrations of the eucharist (particularly, but not exclusively, in the Roman Catholic Church) embody female subordination at the same time that they model human equality around Christ's table. Female subordination is not the only moral failing apparent as Christians gather around the eucharistic table; de facto racial segregation is often apparent, too. Yet, the eucharist stands in contradiction to all the moral failings of the worship community that gathers to celebrate it. The eucharist also represents our joining in the radically inclusive table fellowship of Jesus and our faith in the reign of God/dess symbolized as an abundant banquet at which *all* humanity is filled with good things. The solidarity symbolized and created at the eucharist is an important potential source for the energy to struggle for economic justice for all under conditions of paradoxical prosperity.

The eucharist provides a moral horizon against which Christians can more clearly recognize the darker underside of the dynamic United States economy and of the employability contract that now seems appropriate, given fierce competition throughout the global capitalist system. It is unclear that the employability contract will be a good bargain for workers, except for a small number from the knowledge/managerial elites. If the employability contract is to be morally defensible as a model for the terms of employment for *most* workers, then the communal dimension of employability must receive far greater attention. Both employers and the larger society will have to become genuine partners with workers so that workers can obtain and maintain skills that will make them employable in the global labor markets of the information age. A eucharist-centered spirituality should prod Christians to ask whether the new job contract does provide genuine economic security, and, if so, for whom.

1

A Loss of Employment Security

In the United States in 1998, despite seven years of economic expansion, there are many workers who have a diminished sense of economic security compared to workers several decades ago. In the period from the 1940s through the early 1970s, many United States employers promised their workers jobs with decent salaries and good benefits. If a worker performed adequately, that worker could expect a long-term, although indefinite, tenure with the employer. While factory workers might face layoffs during economic downturns, they could expect to be recalled when the economy revived. White-collar workers rarely faced layoffs. Major United States employers offered implicit long-term employment security to workers who possessed adequate work skills, worked hard, and were loyal to the company. Now, many corporations insist upon greater flexibility to reduce staffing as necessary to remain competitive and to enhance profitability. Increasingly, employers offer, at best, challenging work with a good salary and benefits, but no guarantee of future employment. Indeed, mergers and competitive pressures have led numerous employers to eliminate many jobs entirely.

There is an employment crisis in many of the advanced European nations as well. However, given the nature of their employment systems, labor market pain is distributed differently. In Europe, the workers who are already employed are often protected from job loss. However, the economies of countries like Germany and France have been unable to generate an adequate number of new jobs. In the period from 1970 to 1994, while North America generated forty million new jobs in private industry, the nations of the European Union actually *lost* jobs in the private sector. *The Economist* reports that in the European Union, "the record is dreadful: each recovery has failed to regain the ground lost to unemployment in the previous recession."[1] In fact, despite strong policies protecting jobs, major German companies have actually eliminated jobs and closed plants in their home country.[2]

Thus, one important root of lingering economic anxiety among workers is increased turbulence in labor markets over the last two decades. In the United States, a protracted period of corporate downsizing, which extended for years into the economic expansion of the 1990s, has been especially hard on workers' sense of economic security. The American Management Association reports that almost one quarter of the major U.S. corporations that they surveyed have eliminated jobs in *three or more* of the years following January 1990.[3]

Throughout most of the 1990s, many American workers have been worried about losing their jobs even though the economy was growing. Indeed, in a national survey in 1996, 79 percent of respondents said that "every time" they heard about "a company downsizing" they worried about their own job or that of someone they cared about.[4] Another survey of workers employed by more than four hundred large companies found that the percentage of workers who agreed with the statement "I am frequently concerned about being laid off" rose sharply from 1990 to a peak in 1995. After 1994, the percentage of respondents who often worried about losing their jobs leveled off at 46 percent of respondents.[5] In the summer of 1996, at a time when unemployment was low, 25 percent of the respondents to a Gallup poll still said that they were worried about losing their jobs within six months.[6] Indeed, Alan Greenspan, the chairman of the Federal Reserve Board, has declared that "job insecurity" has been a major factor in holding down workers' wage demands throughout much of the 1990s despite high corporate profits and a protracted economic expansion.

Ordinary Americans have been shaken by two highly publicized types of corporate labor cutbacks. First was a series of large layoffs at several U.S. corporations that had well-known commitments to preserve employees' jobs, even through cyclical downturns. When international competition and industry changes forced companies like Eastman Kodak, Intel, and IBM to lay off workers, the American labor force felt a seismic shift. The second trend that has hit American workers hard recently has been a wave of downsizing by highly profitable corporations, which has continued throughout the economic recovery after the recession of 1990–91. In this decade, less than 20 percent of the firms eliminating jobs showed an operating loss in the year when they shed workers.[7] Workers in the United States are getting the message loud and clear that their jobs are not safe, even when their employers are making solid profits and the overall economy is expanding.

It is important to note that some groups of Americans, particularly workers from socially disadvantaged racial and ethnic groups, have been grappling with job losses and a high degree of employment instability for a long time without sustained public concern or high-profile media attention. Job loss and economic anxiety became big news in the mid-1990s because a large number of middle-level, white-collar jobs held by whites were eliminated in the early years of the decade.

Changes in Job Tenure in a Turbulent Labor Market

To some extent, employment turbulence is a regular condition of the American economy. In any capitalist economy, some jobs are always being destroyed while others are being created. New technologies eliminate positions operating older equipment; a popular new product wipes out the jobs of those who produced the item it replaces; misguided labor union actions or poor management decisions lead to serious job losses. Economists Steven Davis, John Haltiwanger, and Scott Schuh have studied the phenomenon of what they call "job reallocation" in the manufacturing sector during the years 1973 to 1988. They report "nearly one in five manufacturing jobs are either destroyed or created over an average twelve-month interval."[8] One of their important findings is that during the 1970s and 1980s, even in years when net employment remained stable or grew, a large number of jobs were lost. For several decades, there has been substantial turbulence underlying even positive employment figures. According to this study, a sizable proportion of the manufacturing jobs destroyed during the 1970s and 1980s were the least-well-paying jobs. Job loss was also higher in plants that were in the bottom one fifth in terms of wages paid. Thus, less-well-paying jobs with less-well-paying employers were more insecure. The researchers describe their findings as consistent with other research indicating a disproportionate loss of manufacturing jobs for less-skilled workers.[9]

While these three researchers relied on data concerning the manufacturing sector, they refer to other studies that show that the rates of job creation and job destruction are similar in other sectors of the economy.[10] Moreover, Davis, Haltiwanger, and Schuh point out international data showing that "other market economies exhibit comparable rates of job reallocation activity."[11] This research team concludes: "According to the international evidence, the constant churning of job opportunities that characterizes the U.S. labor market represents the normal state of affairs for both developed and developing market economies" in a global capitalist system.[12]

Davis and his colleagues did find one important difference in the job displacement process in more recent years. In the 1970s, job loss in the manufacturing sector included more *temporary layoffs*. Thus, manufacturing workers had a chance to return to jobs that had been temporarily suspended during economic downturns. In the 1980s, dismissals were more likely to be *permanent*. Plant managers were less likely to rehire workers from "layoffs" (at least, within a period of two years). These researchers report that "the recessions of the 1980s involved more restructuring [with permanent loss of jobs in the manufacturing sector] than did the recession of the 1970s."[13] In addition, many of the jobs lost permanently in the recessions of the 1980s were jobs in the larger, higher-paying factories.[14] Davis, Haltiwanger, and Schuh's data carried them up to 1988, but other studies reported in this book indicate that restructuring involving permanent job losses, rather than temporary layoffs, continued to accelerate into the 1990s.

The permanent loss of well-paying manufacturing jobs has hit a segment of the male labor force hard. The job prospects of several groups of men, particularly older men or men with less education, are far less bright these days. Throughout the 1990s, many men—particularly men with less education—have lost their hold on *long-term* jobs. Economists call the length of time that a worker has been with the current employer "job tenure." Long job tenure is one facet of employment security.

Reporting on a study from the Employee Benefit Research Institute, *Business Week* indicated that "between 1991 and 1996, median job-tenure levels for men 25 to 64 fell by an average of around 19%. For men 35 to 64, the drop continues a trend that began in the early 1980s, after male job tenure hit a postwar peak."[15] A key expert on job tenure, Henry Farber, reports that the decline in median job duration among male workers reflects primarily a loss of long-term jobs among men with a high school education or less.[16]

The loss of longer-term job tenure for some men is a factor contributing to growing wage inequalities. Researchers at the Economic Policy Institute explain: "Since the acquisition of job-specific skills is a key source of improved earnings opportunities for most workers (especially those without a college degree), the decline in the share of men with long job tenure has important implications for wage inequality and overall wage growth."[17]

The story is quite different when we turn to women. Women (particularly well-educated women) have gained important ground with respect to job tenure. Henry Farber declares that a long career with the same firm used to be an almost exclusively male prerogative. He indicates that the most striking underlying trend in job tenure data is "the dramatically increased probability of long-term employment for women."[18]

Thus, there are important gender crosscurrents affecting the long-term job tenure of American workers. Women workers have been increasing the time they spend working for the same employer. Henry Farber found that the duration of women's jobs had increased over the period from 1981 to 1993. A recent government study shows that women have continued to gain ground where job tenure is concerned. "Among women, overall median tenure rose between 1983 and 1996, with nearly all of the gain taking place from 1991 to 1996." As more women view their wage labor as a long-term commitment, many women are retaining jobs longer. I believe this is one reason for "substantial increases in median tenure among [female] 35- to 44-year-olds and 45- to 54-year-olds."[19]

The same trend—women gaining ground while men lose ground—is found if researchers focus on those workers who have *lengthy job tenure.* "The proportion of men who had worked for the current employer 10 years or longer fell during the 1983–96 period, while the proportion of women with such long tenure rose." This report continues: "The decline in the proportion of men with such long tenure occurred in every age group, except among men age 65 and over. . . . Among women, the trend toward rising proportions with long tenure occurred mainly among 40- to 54-year-olds."[20]

According to a 1996 Bureau of Labor Statistics report, there were only slight differences between white and black workers in the percentage who had been with the same employer for ten years or more. However, Hispanic workers were significantly less likely than non-Hispanic workers to have been employed by the same employer for ten years or more. Hispanic men's profile compared especially unfavorably to that of other male workers.[21]

This data on job tenure is very suggestive of a growing economic insecurity, particularly for men with less education. However, Department of Labor researchers offer an important caution about drawing conclusions about job security based on statistics about job tenure. They point out that median job tenure often *rises* during the typical recession when jobs are less secure. "During recession or other periods of declining job security, median tenure and the proportion of workers with long tenure could rise because less-senior workers are more likely to lose their jobs than are workers with longer tenure. During periods of economic growth, median tenure . . . could fall because . . . experienced workers have more opportunities to change employers and take better jobs."[22]

STRAINS ON EMPLOYMENT SECURITY INCREASE

Throughout the 1990s, there has been a series of other signals that employment security has been under greater pressure than during other post–World War II decades. First, according to Farber, although the recession of 1990–91 was a relatively mild one, jobs were destroyed at a higher rate than during the more severe recession of 1981–83. He suggests: "This is very preliminary evidence consistent with the view that there has been a secular decline in job security."[23] Even more ominously, job losses continued at a relatively high level in the first two years of the economic expansion that began in 1991.

Even as late July 1995–June 1996, when the U.S. economy had been expanding for many years, a large number of major corporations were still eliminating jobs. According to the American Management Association, almost half of the corporations they surveyed had eliminated jobs during that period. However, the term "downsizing" did not necessarily apply, since many corporations were creating new jobs in some areas while abolishing positions in other areas. In fact, in the 1995–96 period, the number of jobs destroyed by large corporations was only slightly greater than the number of jobs created by those same companies. According to the American Management Association, companies with ten thousand employees or more eliminated more jobs than they created, and such companies were the most likely to have actually "downsized" in 1995–96.[24] AMA researchers report: "At the time the 1996 AMA survey was taken, the U.S. economy was in the sixth year of ongoing expansion; nevertheless, nearly one-third of surveyed companies employ fewer workers today than in January 1990. Half of the survey's largest firms (employing 10,000 or more workers) have actually downsized since that date."[25]

An analysis sponsored by *The New York Times* of U.S. Labor Department data confirmed that job losses remained severe as late as 1995—four years into an economic expansion. Reporter Steve Lohr indicates that

> the number of people laid off in 1995 . . . rose to nearly the peak reached in 1992, right after the last recession. Through November of [1996], even after more than five years of economic recovery, the number of layoffs announced by companies had increased 14 percent from a year earlier. . . .
>
> The new findings confirm that layoffs have become a durable fixture of today's economy, occurring steadily in good times and bad.[26]

It was not until 1996–97 that the American Management Association survey on job creation and job elimination showed that large firms were creating many more jobs than they were eliminating. Even then, almost one in five major companies was still downsizing, that is, cutting more jobs than they added.[27]

In addition, during the 1990s more of those who lost their jobs indicated that their positions were completely abolished, rather than that they were laid off temporarily because of "slack work." In the past, workers who were laid off due to "slack work" stood a chance to be called back to the job when the economy resumed growing and demand increased. Now, a larger portion of those displaced from their jobs, both men and women, say that their old jobs have ceased to exist.

Findings in the 1996 AMA survey tend to confirm that an increasing proportion of the workers who lose their jobs are losing them because their companies are abolishing positions permanently as they downsize or "reengineer" their business processes.[28] The percentage of survey respondents who select automation as a cause of job elimination in this survey steadily increased since 1991–92. In 1995–96, 20 percent of the respondents cited automation as a reason for eliminating jobs. In fact, "automation or other technological processes is the biggest gainer [as a rationale for job elimination]."[29] An AMA news release states: "The findings indicate that restructuring, reengineering, and new technologies are far more likely to cost jobs than create them. Job elimination tends to be structural; job creation remains tied to the business cycle."[30]

In the 1990s, job loss hit white-collar workers in the United States harder than ever before. In absolute numbers, more white-collar workers than blue-collar workers lost jobs during the period from 1991 to 1993. (However, *proportionally* more blue-collar workers were displaced.)[31] According to one recent study, more than 10 percent of men with a college education—those most likely to hold good white-collar jobs—were fired during those years.[32] While job loss hit men with less education especially hard, during the period from 1981 to 1993, the rate of job loss grew among men with more education, too.[33] Another study of employment in the 100 largest U.S. corporations over the last decade and a half concluded that 22 percent of the employees of those companies had been laid off and that the vast majority of those losing work over this period had been white-collar workers.[34]

Henry Farber's review of government data shows that displaced workers with more education were more likely to report that their previous position had been abolished. Farber says that permanent job loss "grew primarily and substantially in the higher educational categories (at least some college). This is consistent with reports of elimination of substantial numbers of white collar jobs in some large organizations."[35] In addition, Farber's analysis shows that, in the mid-1990s, managers suffered from serious job turbulence. He concludes that in the period ending in 1993: "The most dramatic change in job loss rates occurs for managers and workers in sales and administration. Rates of job loss for managers show a substantial increase from their 1987–89 level, and job loss due to 'position abolished' accounts for all (and more) of this increase. This is consistent with reports that corporations are reorganizing in ways that eliminate the jobs of significant numbers of managerial workers."[36]

Still, in the mid-1990s, workers who lost a job because their employer abolished the position were more likely to find new jobs than were workers who lost their jobs for other reasons like slack work. College-educated workers were also more likely to find new jobs within the survey period.[37] In the period 1989–93, nonwhites were more likely than whites to lose their jobs. Their job loss was more likely to be the result of "slack work" than because their position had been abolished. Nonwhites were 15 percent less likely to find new jobs.[38]

In recent years, female workers have been less likely than male workers to be displaced. Still, over the last fifteen years, the percentage of women among displaced workers *has* risen. In part, this reflects "a shift in the distribution of industries from which workers lost jobs."[39] In the early 1990s, the displacement rate grew in sales and in finance and insurance—economic sectors that employ a larger share of women. Once women are displaced, they are more likely to be reemployed on a part-time (not full-time) basis. Farber found that this remained true even after he took into account the fact that women workers generally are more likely to be working part-time than men. Since a portion of the women who lost full-time jobs were more likely than their male counterparts to settle for part-time employment, Farber suggested that "this result is unlikely to be primarily the result of [women's] preferences."[40] Women displaced from their jobs are also less likely to find new jobs than are men, and they are more likely to leave the labor force completely.[41]

A significant segment of the workers who lose their jobs suffer a serious loss of income, even after they find new jobs. Throughout the 1990s, about half of all workers who lost full-time jobs and who were reemployed in other full-time positions received new wages that were equal to, or better than, their wages in the prior job.

About half of the workers could not find standard full-time positions or found full-time jobs at reduced wages. Recent data on the period from 1993 to 1995—a period of economic growth—showed that "about one-third [of displaced workers now reemployed in other, full-time positions] suffered earnings losses of 20 percent or more."[42] In addition, almost 25 percent of displaced workers who had been covered by health insurance on their previous job were not covered by an employer-sponsored health plan on their new jobs.[43] Reviewing the period from 1981 to 1993, Henry Farber indicates that workers who were displaced because their former positions were abolished faced an increasing risk of serious financial loss. Surveying data covering a decade, he reports that earnings losses suffered by these workers have been growing steadily since 1983.[44] Particularly disturbing is some information that suggests that displaced female workers who do find new jobs can be hit especially hard by reduced wages. Adam Seitchik reports that "in percentage terms the loss was much larger for married women and female family heads than it was for married men."[45]

MARGINALIZED WORKERS—THOSE OVER 54

Even experts who stress the power of the United States economy to create new jobs agree that one *new* social group is suffering as a result of increased labor market turbulence. That group is male workers over the age of 54. Indeed a particularly attractive way to cut the workforce, especially in the initial stages of the downsizing era, was to offer appealing, voluntary, early retirement plans. More recently, older workers, particularly workers in corporations that have already been through a previous downsizing effort, find a so-called voluntary retirement proposal to be an offer one "can't refuse." Some workers perceive a lightly concealed threat that those who do not retire voluntarily today will be terminated with a less generous severance package tomorrow.

Job tenure data provides evidence that a growing number of men over 54 have been pushed out of jobs they had held for many years, and sometimes pushed out of the labor market entirely. Henry Farber found that male workers 55 to 64 years old experienced declining job tenure in the period from 1981 to 1993. According to Farber, this reflects "the move toward earlier retirement."[46] According to the Bureau of Labor Statistics, the decline in job duration for older men has continued through 1996. "Particularly sharp drops" in median job tenure have occurred "among men ages 45 to 54 and 55 to 64." The drop was steepest for men 55 to 64. In 1983 the median number of years with the present employer for men in this age group was 15.3; in 1991, it was 13.4; in 1996, it was 10.5.[47] Thus, the drop in job tenure continued throughout the sustained economic expansion that began in 1991. An Employee Benefit Research Institute report also showed that job tenure of older men continued to drop significantly for more than a decade. "Since 1983, median job tenure has dropped by 6 years, or 29%, among males 55 to 64."[48]

In the last two recessions, a large number of middle-aged men lost their jobs. In addition, the trend accelerated over the last decade. "Between 1981 and 1983, ten per cent of men between forty-five and fifty-four and eleven per cent of men between fifty-five and sixty-four got laid off. . . . Ten years later, in 1991–93, the . . . job-loss rates for these two groups rose to fourteen per cent and seventeen per cent respectively."[49] Among male workers, the youngest workers are still more likely to lose their jobs during recessionary periods. However, in the early years of the 1990s, older male workers suffered an unprecedented degree of job loss. Farber indicates: "For men in the three groups comprising workers 35–64 years old, job loss rates are higher after 1989 than even in the deep recession of the early 1980's. Job loss rates have risen substantially for older men. While similar patterns are found for women, . . . there are much smaller distinctions across age groups and the changes over time are much smaller for women."[50]

Many men in their late fifties and early sixties find that they are unprepared financially and psychologically for permanent retirement. Therefore, they search for other jobs. In 1993, Henry Farber reported that only people over 54 were still having a hard time finding new jobs.[51] In 1996, a story in *Fortune* described the man over 54 as "the person . . . with the least chance of finding new employment that comes close to matching his old job."[52] Even as the economy was finally creating a significant number of new jobs (by February 1996), men over 54 who had lost their jobs were still finding it harder than their younger male peers to get new positions. Thirteen percent were unemployed and 27 percent had left the labor force.[53]

Older workers, ages 55–64, who lost their jobs were also more likely to work part-time if they succeeded in finding a new job. Researcher Henry Farber suggests that older workers have sought part-time positions "perhaps reflecting a move toward partial retirement."[54] However, I suggest that it might also reflect fewer full-time options for older, displaced workers.

Still, as the demand for labor has increased in the late 1990s, older men who had left the labor force found new job opportunities open to them. In 1995, the labor force participation rate for men 55–64 began to rise after a long period of decline. The movement of older men back into this strong labor market suggests that men over 55 wanted to work but had trouble finding and keeping jobs in the first half of the 1990s.[55]

My discussion up to this point has been about middle-aged men, but some government statistics suggest that middle-aged women who lose their jobs are facing problems even more severe than their male age-peers. However, these women are not drawing the attention of commentators on the economy. Perhaps there has been less attention to the plight of middle-aged, female displaced workers because there have been fewer of them. In the period 1991–93, men were overrepresented among displaced workers, mainly because men were also overrepresented "in industries, such as manufacturing, that have high rates of displacement."[56] However, men were also more likely than women to find new jobs after they lost their previous positions. Both these trends continued throughout the years 1993 to 1995. During the economic recovery of the mid-1990s, only 41 percent of displaced female workers ages 55–64 were reemployed; 22 percent were unemployed and 37 percent had left the labor force. (In comparison, 61 percent of the men in their age cohort were reemployed; 13 percent were unemployed; and 27 percent were out of the labor force.) In fact, in the mid-1990s, the reemployment rate among these women *fell below* their reemployment rate in 1991–93. Middle-aged women's unemployment rate remained stable; the additional nonemployed older female workers left the labor force. In the 1990s, a woman who loses her job after age 54 has less than a fifty-fifty chance of finding a new job.[57] No one seems to be paying attention to the situation faced by these older women, however.

The ranks of people in their late fifties and early sixties who are "in early retirement" are swelling in European nations, as well as in the United States. In fact, some European countries make special social welfare provisions to supplement the income of displaced workers who take "early retirement." Governments do this in order to open up jobs for the large number of unemployed young people in those countries. One author says, "In western Europe a strong sentiment exists that . . . the economy cannot and will not in the foreseeable future be able to generate sufficient jobs for all those who might want them. That being the case, there is a feeling that older workers have an obligation to withdraw from the labor force to make way for younger workers."[58]

While more years of leisure at the end of life may sound positive, there is a social problem brewing with early retirement that has not yet been widely acknowledged. This accelerating pattern of early retirements raises a number of social questions. With a rise in life expectancy, can society provide adequate economic support for large numbers of men and women through an even more protracted period of "retirement," stretching from early retirement through death at a later age? Does the plight of older white men—who are socially privileged by virtue of their gender and race but vulnerable to employer bias because of age—represent a warning sign? In a fiercely competitive global environment, will larger numbers of white men be squeezed out of the labor market, as many of their black male counterparts have already been? Is the growth of early retirement masking the early signs that the economy can rarely come close to providing enough full-time jobs for all those who want jobs, even though the United States is experiencing "miraculous" levels of job creation?

JOB CREATION IN A "DYNAMIC" UNITED STATES ECONOMY

Many commentators, surveying the United States economy today, stress the enviable ability of the U.S. economy *to create large numbers of new jobs*. During the same week that *The New York Times* was running an unprecedented series titled "The Downsizing of America," the White House was holding a news conference to announce that between 1993 and 1996 the U.S. economy had generated 8.4 million net new jobs.[59] (By November 1997, the economy had created 13.5 million net new jobs.)[60]

The large number of new jobs that were created in the second half of the 1990s were slow in coming considering the economic cycle. In 1994, a number of observers were calling the economic scene a "jobless recovery." However, as the economic expansion continued, the number and the quality of jobs increased. In mid-decade, federal officials reported with pride that "since January of 1994, seventy-six percent of all net new jobs created have been in managerial and professional sectors."[61] Rebutting critics who charged that the United States economy was creating a large number of bad jobs—that is, jobs that are low-wage and insecure—government officials pointed out that job growth in the professional and managerial sectors suggests that most of the net new jobs are higher-wage jobs. Job growth has also been higher in the industries that traditionally pay well.

An economist commissioned by *The New York Times* to analyze the quality of newly created jobs found that, in 1995, "45 percent of the jobs created across the country . . . paid more than the national average wage." In addition, "fully one-quarter paid more than 30 percent above the average." Economist Mark Zandi commented, "We're seeing a lot of job growth in sectors and occupations that are high-paying."[62]

However, economists at the Economic Policy Institute have questioned analyses praising the high quality of jobs created in the United States economy since the mid-1990s. Jeff Faux asserts that the job expansion has been largely in the service sector. He contends that "most of the gains have been in the low-wage retail trade and consumer services sectors."[63] He also points out that the proportion of workers receiving health insurance and pension plan coverage has declined.

The unemployment rate in the United has been below 6 percent since September 1994. By fall 1997, it fell below 5 percent and unemployment figures were the lowest they had been in a quarter century. In 1994, despite the fact that inflation was remarkably low, some economists began to warn that the labor market was now so tight that there was bound to be upward pressure on wages.[64] Indeed, since late 1995, wages have risen modestly. However, profits have risen substantially throughout the extended expansion in the United States economy during the 1990s. Investors have reaped the lion's share of the wealth created throughout this expansion. The average worker had to wait a long time to see the fruits of the expansion in his or her paycheck. When wages finally increased, the increase (adjusted for inflation) was relatively small.

During a White House news conference on March 8, 1996, Joseph Stiglitz, chair of the Council of Economic Advisors, was asked why there was so much economic anxiety among Americans when the economy had been growing for years and job growth has been substantial. Stiglitz replied that the United States had "an extremely dynamic economy."[65] While a lot of jobs were being created, a lot of other jobs were being destroyed. He conceded that there was a lot of what he called "job transition," what I would call job "displacement or dislocation." "Job transition" or "job dislocation" is a phenomenon increasingly experienced by even privileged workers in the United States economy. Over the last ten years, managerial workers have experienced a growing amount of job dislocation, but paradoxically, as a group, managerial workers have also experienced one of the highest rates of job growth.

THE DISLOCATION OF MIDDLE MANAGEMENT

As we have seen, there has been substantial turbulence in the managerial labor force throughout this decade. However, as the economy expanded, the managerial sector of the labor force has replaced the jobs lost during the recession of 1990–91. Job loss at the management level has been proportionally worse than in previous years, but job creation has been proportionally better. Among companies reporting to the Equal Employment Opportunity Commission in 1994, the number of managers was "almost unchanged" from the total in 1990. *Wall Street Journal* writer Alex Markels reports: "Despite years of relentless downsizing, 'right-sizing' and re-engineering in corporate America, all aimed in part at shedding excess bureaucracy, reports of middle management's demise are proving much exaggerated."[66]

The largest corporations in the United States *have* actually reduced their overall managerial workforces since 1989. And the elimination of middle management positions by major corporations has continued as a strong pattern throughout the 1990s. According to the AMA in 1996, while middle managers were 8 percent of the workforce, they were 20 percent of the workers whose jobs were eliminated in the businesses surveyed.[67] Moreover, "almost three middle management jobs were cut for every one created."[68]

In some cases, highly visible reductions at the middle management level by these large corporations generated unprecedented media coverage. However, over the same period, smaller enterprises have collectively been creating a large number of new managerial positions. "Companies employing fewer than 20,000 U.S. workers have added about 180,000 management jobs since 1989. The biggest growth is at companies with 10,000 to 20,000 employees."[69]

During the present recovery, the proportion of managerial and professional jobs has grown in relation to manufacturing and clerical jobs. Economist Paul Osterman points out that "restructuring may have caused a reduction in middle managers at companies, but it's often increased their percentage of the total work force."[70] For example, when a company outsources maintenance, data processing, or manufacturing work, it often retains executives who define projects, coordinate relationships with outside sources, and monitor the results. In addition, as routine blue- and white-collar tasks are automated, a proportionally larger number of the remaining jobs require a higher level of judgment. If the corporation has a program to evaluate regularly the skill level of positions and to rationalize job titles and salaries in accord with the skill and judgment required, then some redesigned "production" jobs— now requiring increased judgment—are reassigned to technical, professional, or managerial categories. In addition, the global activities of many businesses are growing. One source suggested to Markels that a larger cadre of senior executives is needed to set policy for and to oversee growing global enterprises.

There is another interesting potential explanation for managerial job growth. Markels indicates that historically white-collar workers have been supervised by a larger corps of managers than comparable numbers of blue-collar workers. Since the proportion of the workforce engaged in white-collar work has grown, there is a historical trend toward growth at the managerial level. Markels continues: "In addition, as white-collar jobs become more sophisticated, the number of managers required tends to grow."[71]

Economist David Gordon, in *Fat and Mean: The Corporate Squeeze of Working Americans and the Myth of Managerial "Downsizing,"*[72] argued that a large number of managerial positions have been created to supervise the output of "production" workers who, presently, have little incentive to work hard in the absence of such close monitoring. He pointed out that the real wage increases enjoyed by production-level workers during the 1950s and 1960s evaporated after 1973. Workers no longer believed that hard work and greater productivity would translate into real wage increases, so they had little reason to "give their all" on the job. Gordon suggested that corporations have responded by ending job security and increasing supervisory/managerial monitoring of workers. Fear of job loss and a sense that "the boss is always watching" convinced employees to work hard throughout the day. While Gordon made the questionable assumption that most of those employees classified as managers had significant supervisory roles, his thesis deserves consideration.

An economic paradox remains. During the 1990s in the United States, "layoffs"—which actually mean the permanent elimination of jobs—have become commonplace, cutting a wider swath across the working and middle classes. Since the middle of the decade, however, the same economy has been creating an unprecedented number of new jobs. As economist Paul Krugman commented in 1996, "What economists call 'labor market flexibility' is a euphemism for a certain amount of brutality. But it seems to be an unfortunate price we have to pay for having as dynamic an economy as we do."[73] Krugman acknowledges the pain that accompanies job dislocation, but he makes it seem unavoidable. Perhaps it is the result of some unchangeable economic force. But as an ethicist, I contend that the "brutality" of our flexible economy could be mitigated and that there is a moral obligation to search for ways to do so. In the more flexible economy of the 1990s, there is a new implicit job contract. It is past time that society began to evaluate morally the terms of that new job contract.

2

The picture of the United States as a dynamic economy that is creating more jobs than are being destroyed—particularly for managerial and professional workers—fits well with the growing chorus of voices that are urging that workers shift their expectations from job security toward "employability."

Some of those surveying the employment scene in the United States contend that employers are presenting workers with a new employment bargain. A fundamental element in the "new employment contract" is a new provision for the worker's long-term economic security. The employer no longer promises long-term employment with the company (contingent upon acceptable job performance by the employee). Indeed, many employers say that under highly competitive conditions in an increasingly deregulated, global economy, the employer *cannot honestly make promises of long-term employment*. Instead, what the company offers the employee is an opportunity to utilize and to enhance work skills that will make the employee a strong competitor in the external labor market—should the present employment relationship be terminated. Many commentators call having highly marketable work skills "employability." Employers thus promise to provide workers with an opportunity to develop and continually upgrade their "employability."

Sociologist Charles Heckscher provides the following picture of this new employment relationship: "In this conception, *to*

sketch its ideal form, individuals are committed not to any company as such, but to a personal set of skills, goals, interests, and affiliations. The company offers them not permanent employment, but challenges that give them an opportunity to develop their interests, and a promise of mutual dialogue and openness to manage
. . . [corporate requirements and the individual's career] needs."[1]

Heckscher is one of a growing chorus of voices who are urging workers to shift their expectations from employment security with a particular employer toward "employability" in a dynamic labor market. Talk of employability suggests that, from now on, savvy employees (and their families) will achieve a reasonable degree of economic security by maintaining (as individuals) a high level of economically valuable skills. According to this view, a worker who has good skills can be confident that he or she will find another job with a good salary and benefits quickly if his or her present job is terminated. This strand in the discussion of employability emphasizes that individuals should take personal responsibility for maintaining their employment skills in a constantly changing labor market.

Under the "employability" model, each worker is an entrepreneur constantly seeking out opportunities—on the job and elsewhere—to improve his or her employment prospects. The worker possesses a portfolio of marketable labor skills and the worker, as an individual, should always be on the lookout for opportunities to upgrade that portfolio. Thus, there is a highly individualistic thrust to this model. The individual worker must give high priority to managing and upgrading his or her personal skills.

Since each worker's economic security depends on possessing a highly marketable portfolio of skills, then relationships with others in the workplace become more complex. Fellow workers are engaged in pursuing organizational goals through cooperative effort. However, at the same time, each worker is maneuvering to get those assignments that contribute the most to the individual worker's set of skills. There will inevitably be times when promoting one's interests alienates co-workers or conflicts with the best interests of the organization. Certainly, there have always been ambitious employees who put their personal advancement ahead of the welfare of their co-workers or the best interests of the organization. What is new under the employability model is that such self-serving efforts are explicitly recommended. Each worker's economic security now more clearly depends on giving priority to developing one's individual job skills. Many contemporary religious ethicists stress the importance of human relationality. Such a positive view of relationality is in tension with the thrust of the "employability" model. This tension is reflected in the advice that Harvard Business School professor Daniel Quinn Mills offers employees. He urges that they adopt a more provisional attitude toward their relationships with their fellow workers and their present employer. Mills recommends not developing strong friendships with co-workers, in part because emotional ties may blind employees to early signs that their current job is threatened by business conditions and that they should be actively looking for a new position outside the current company. At the same time, Mills suggests cultivating good relationships with people in the same field who work at other companies. When the time comes to leave the present job, those outside contacts may prove invaluable in a job search. In an "employability" environment, each employee is an individual who will be tempted to take a strictly instrumental view of workplace relationships. The key question becomes "How will this relationship enable me to become a more valuable commodity on the external labor market?"

Several writers have suggested that all workers will become more like those professional employees for whom peer relationships, inside and outside the company, have long been crucial. Indeed, Heckscher urges middle managers, on whom he focuses, to adopt a "professional" model of the employment relationship. By this, he means that managers should give more attention to upgrading their skills in comparison with peers throughout the labor market. Using one's occupational peer group as a crucial performance benchmark means, Heckscher suggests, acting like professionals who create a relatively secure niche in the workplace by maintaining high-level skills when compared with fellow professionals across the nation and, perhaps, the globe. The employability model suggests *all* workers will depend less on their identity as employees of Exxon, AT&T, or IBM and more on their pride as top performers among their peer group.

I think that Heckscher's decision to use the professions as a key analogy for the new employment relationship is understandable. As I examine the "employability" model, it seems to "fit" best precisely for some highly skilled professionals, especially for technical experts in highly fluid, "hi-tech" environments. For example, I contend that the following description of the consequences of the new employment contract reflects most accurately the situation of certain highly skilled professionals who work in rapidly changing environments. Heckscher says: "The match between individual and organization is a temporary one, defined by the *frame of the project* or mission. The fact that you have done your best for twenty years is not the point, and entails no obligation on the part of the company; contributing to the current direction of the firm is what matters."[2]

This less secure, but more challenging, employment future may seem stimulating to workers with highly desirable "knowledge" skills. Rosabeth Moss Kanter points out that such knowledge experts have "skills and reputation—that can be invested in new opportunities as they arise." She predicts: "No matter what changes take place, persons whose pool of intellectual capital or expertise is high are in a better position to find gainful employment—with the current company, with another company, or on their own." For these elite workers, "Companies come and go, but technical know-how can still find a home."[3]

Kanter describes as exciting the prospects open to those who possess the top skills in demand in a global market. She says that such individuals are a part of the emerging "world class." Kanter explains: "'World class' is a play on words suggesting both the need to meet the highest standards anywhere in order to compete and the growth of a social class defined by its ability to command resources and operate beyond borders and across wide territories."[4] She continues, "At one extreme of the cosmopolitan class is a small global elite of business leaders creating powerful, border-spanning networks. These cosmopolitans have unlimited opportunities because of their ability to tap resources or gain access to knowledge anywhere in the world."[5] The world-class, knowledge elite will be the big winners under the new employability model. World-class professionals and managers can sell their top skills to employers or clients across the globe for enormous salaries or fees.

Much smaller rewards or even economic penalties will be the lot of the majority of workers whose skills do not put them in the top tier or who, for other reasons, cannot peddle their skills in a global labor market. Social critic Jeremy Rifkin sees the much darker underside of Kanter's vision of the future for world-class individuals. Rifkin warns: "The information and communications technologies and global market forces are fast polarizing the world's population into two irreconcilable and potentially warring forces—a new cosmopolitan elite of 'symbolic analysts' who control the technologies and the forces of production, and the growing numbers of permanently displaced workers who have little hope and even fewer prospects for meaningful employment in the new high-tech global economy."[6] While Rifkin's view is somewhat apocalyptic, there are serious questions about how and why employers would provide challenging workplace opportunities that make lower-echelon workers—or even the "average" worker—highly employable in the external labor market.

An op-ed piece in *The New York Times* suggests another problem with an employability paradigm rooted in the experience of high-tech workers who are in high demand. As workers grow older it may become more difficult for many of them to maintain cutting-edge skills. Norman Matloff, a computer science professor, alleges that age discrimination is a serious problem in technical computer fields, despite what is currently a very tight market for such skills. He asserts: "High-tech companies save money by shunning most midcareer programmers and focusing their hiring on new or recent college graduates, who are cheaper and can work lots of overtime."[7] Implicit in his complaint is a charge that high-tech firms are not living up to an employability contract. They are not consistently providing existing workers with opportunities to learn new computer languages and other skills that make them highly employable within the field of computer science. If Matloff's anecdotal account is accurate, the employability model may be inadequate to provide employment security, particularly for older workers.

CORPORATE RESPONSIBILITY AND WORKER "EMPLOYABILITY"

While individuals are challenged to take more responsibility for the direction of their careers under the "employability contract," there are also key corporate responsibilities. Under this model, the corporation no longer promises to preserve jobs. Rather, the company promises to give employees the opportunity to enhance their skills in their present jobs, so that the employees will have valuable skills to offer—even to offer another employer if necessary. Companies that are pioneering in enhancing worker "employability" offer services such as more extensive individual career counseling, mentoring that focuses on skill development, and training at company expense and, perhaps, on company time.

A company is most likely to support skills training if the employee is acquiring or upgrading skills that are directly useful to the current employer. A company's commitment to enhance its workers' "employability" is tested when an employee believes that he or she would benefit from training or a change in job duties that, in the opinion of management, is not likely to benefit the company directly over the short run. Economist Eileen Appelbaum cautions that when employee training is in question, "rational calculations of the firm's ability to capture the returns to such investment [in training] lead to an overemphasis on providing workers with narrow, firm-specific skills."[8] This is probably particularly true for lower-level service and clerical workers and for production workers in certain manufacturing companies. For such workers, the limited, firm-specific skills training that companies can most easily "cost-justify" are the very skills that do little or nothing to make a worker more "employable" in the eyes of another company. In addition, Appelbaum warns: "Numerous studies have shown that race, gender, and amount of formal education are important determinants of who receives . . . [employer-provided] training in the US."[9] The person who is most likely to get employer-paid training to sharpen his skills is a white male who has more than a high-school education, but he is just the type of worker whose "employability" is already relatively high (as long as he is under fifty-five).

In addition, if the company needs more workers possessing a particular skill *and* if there is a potential labor pool available who *already possess* that skill, it may be more expedient for the company to fire some of its existing workers and to hire other workers who already have the needed capabilities. If the new workers are entry-level workers or younger workers, the company may realize substantial labor cost savings in addition to an immediate application of the new skills. One human resources manager for an electronics firm told Kanter frankly that his company's older workforce was a competitive liability. He confided: "Our average employee has eighteen years of service. If you were starting a new company, you would not hire a fifty-five-year-old at a substantial salary who must be retrained and who comes with higher liabilities and insurance costs."[10] Under the new employment contract, where the fifty-five-year-old worker is promised a job only as long as his or her present skills contribute to the company's mission and immediate goals, it is not clear why the employer has any obligation to offer the older worker a company-sponsored opportunity to be retrained.

Yet, Daniel Mills asserts that under the new "employability" model the opportunity to develop marketable skills is the crucial component promised by employers to employees. He declares that failure to provide every employee with an opportunity for growth in skills constitutes a serious breach of the new contract. He judges that an employer "exploits" an employee if the employer merely benefits from the employee's current abilities without providing opportunities for the employee to enhance those capacities through gaining new experiences and skills. Mills concludes: "In today's rapidly changing world in which up-to-date skills are needed to find and retain jobs, this is unfair to employees."[11]

However, it is not clear what means employers will use to insure that *each* employee has a continuous opportunity to develop economic skills that constantly remain marketable in the external labor market. Economist Lester Thurow has examined the conflicting interests of employee and employer under the new "employability" model of the job contract. He concludes: "Perhaps lifetime employability is workable, but not one company has yet worked out what such a contract would mean and how it would work."[12]

Eileen Appelbaum suggests that in a market economy, social and political institutions will have to impose constraints on investors and their agents in order to uphold employability contracts. She cautions: "Otherwise, firms in competitive markets will have difficulty resisting the temptation to exploit any weakness in the market power of the workforce for short-term advantage, and difficulty justifying the expenditures on investments in the skills and capabilities of front line (production) workers."[13]

A realistic look at the current situation shows that for workers whose skills are more mundane than those of the "knowledge elite" or who are finding it hard to keep their skills on the cutting edge of new social and technical developments, the new employment contract offers an ominous future. Kanter admits, "The global economy is experienced by people across the occupational spectrum as a loss of certainty, a game in which today's success still does not guarantee the future; there is no letup, no stopping, in the pursuit of the next concept and skill."[14] Such relentless demands take no account of the fact that most adult human beings have periods in their lives when it is almost impossible to keep up with unceasing workplace demands. Over a lifetime there are many events that might make it difficult or impossible for a worker to pursue the next skill without any letup. Divorce, the death of a loved one, or learning that one has a serious but treatable disease are all examples of common occurrences that would make it difficult for many employees to engage in a ceaseless drive to maintain their "employability."

Under the prior long-term employment contract, employers often responded compassionately to a temporary decline in productivity experienced by an employee who was known to have a serious personal problem. This was particularly true in the case of a "good worker." Since the employment relationship was a long-term one, the employer could reasonably expect that, over the term of the employment relationship, the contribution of the normally diligent employee would more than compensate the employer for poorer performance during a period of temporary personal stress. Under the new employability contract, where the employee has a job as long as the employee is contributing to the immediate goals of the organization, there is no reason for the employer to be so forbearing. After all, since the term of the employment relationship is tenuous, the employer can no longer be confident that a particular employee's long-term contribution will be a positive one. The employee may be less likely to remain with the company long enough to compensate for the period of lower performance.

EMPLOYABILITY AND ECONOMIC POLARIZATION

The emphasis on individual employability means higher risks, but also potentially higher rewards for some. Those whose personal "employability" is unusually high can expect to command a high price in the external labor market. The former CEO of a Fortune 500 company described the increased competition for the services of the "knowledge elite" well. He said: "Intellectual capital will go where it is wanted, and it will stay where it is well treated."[15] Especially under the "pay for performance" compensation systems that are increasingly popular, the most "employable," most highly skilled workers will command high salaries.

The high compensation rates needed to attract or retain the world's most "employable" workers is one aspect of what economists Robert Frank and Philip Cook have termed "the winner-take-all society." Frank and Cook are disturbed by growing economic disparities in the United States. They attribute a significant part of the nation's growing economic inequalities to the extraordinarily large amounts of wealth that can be demanded by the top performers (the winners) in a wide variety of fields such as athletics, publishing, and corporate management. The two authors point out that advances in communications and transportation technology now mean that the services of the top performers in many fields can be sold to the highest bidders in a global labor market. The services of the world's best entertainers or doctors, for example, command top dollar from the richest individuals or groups across the globe. Frank and Cook suggest that this pattern of inordinate rewards to the few top performers, whose skills may be only marginally better than those of their nearest competitors, replicates itself on a more local scale as well. Economic inequalities are further exacerbated by the large economic rewards given to "'minor-league superstars' who dominate the smaller niche markets of everyday life."[16] I claim that employability as a paradigm for the employment relationship coheres nicely with a winner-take-all mentality. These converging trends suggest that the losses suffered by the losers whose employability is low or dwindling will be quite severe.

DANGERS FOR THE CORPORATION

The new employment contract has some largely unexplored risks for corporations, too. Under the employability model, a company must constantly provide key employees with opportunities to upgrade their skills. However, sometimes companies genuinely need employees to concentrate on mundane duties that require the exercise of existing skills. For example, many companies need computer programmers to make routine changes in existing computer programs that are written in standard computer languages. However, it is often difficult to hire and retain programmers to perform such badly needed work, because these "maintenance" jobs don't allow programmers to gain experience with newer, cutting-edge languages. As the new employability contract becomes more widespread, it may be difficult to recruit employees for a wide range of crucial, but routine, work—work that needs to be done but does not enhance the employee's marketability in the external labor market.

Moreover, if the new employment agreement lasts only as long as it maximizes benefits for each party, key employees are fully entitled to leave as soon as they are offered a better opportunity elsewhere. When labor markets are tight, workers—particularly more skilled workers—have little reason to remain loyal to their present employer. In the second half of the 1990s, there are many places in the United States where unemployment has been quite low and the competition for skilled workers has been keen. Many employers have found to their dismay that it is difficult to retain workers with good skills. In periods when unemployment is low, the employees with the best skills may be even more likely to quit in order to pursue greater opportunities elsewhere.

In a passage that should be chilling for senior executives, Mills advises employees to pursue their own interests ruthlessly if their company faces hard times. He counsels: "When you first sense that a business might be failing, get out." He continues: "Don't wait to be the last off a sinking ship. The first to leave will get the best opportunities elsewhere."[17]

Interestingly, some business experts argue that companies would be *more competitive over the long run* if they found ways to *retain* highly "employable" workers as a reliable, highly motivated, loyal workforce, instead of grooming them to be "employable" by someone else if they are let go. Jeffrey Pfeffer suggests that a knowledgeable workforce can provide a "competitive advantage" in an advanced economy. He concludes, "If the work force is, indeed, an increasingly important source of competitive advantage—then it is important to build a work force that . . . cannot be readily duplicated by others."[18] Lester Thurow agrees that, in an information-based economy, companies would be *more* competitive if they attracted and retained a highly skilled workforce. However, Thurow sees many companies undercutting their workers' sense of security and loyalty, despite the fact that it would be mutually beneficial to enhance ties with skilled employees. Thurow comments: "With brainpower as the only source of strategic competitive advantage, firms should be integrating their skilled workforce ever more tightly into their organizations. But with corporate downsizing, they are doing precisely the opposite."[19]

Other economists have been promoting "functional flexibility" as a more humane and potentially more profitable way for corporations to structure the employment relationship. An organization that promotes functional flexibility offers workers a larger measure of employment security. Economist Robert Boyer, among others, suggests that employees who anticipate secure future employment with a firm will be more willing to develop multifaceted skills, to pitch in to complete a variety of useful tasks, and to cooperate with new projects.[20] Training plays an important part in any drive for functional flexibility because long-time employees often need to develop new skills as the company's operations change. Therefore, companies seeking to provide long-term employment must offer employees repeated opportunities for retraining, in order for their employees to fit into new positions as the company continually transforms itself. As Rosabeth Moss Kanter says: "Even a promise of long-term employment is possible only because of programs aimed at ensuring employability. Companies can offer to invest in retraining and career counseling to upgrade people's skills continually so they will always be employable, although specific jobs might disappear and they might have to prove their ability to contribute to the company over and over again throughout their careers."[21]

Some experts and executives are starting to challenge senior management to demonstrate more creativity in finding ways to cultivate new business opportunities that will keep their existing workforce gainfully employed. Donald Hastings, chief executive officer of Lincoln Electric—a company that still has a no-layoff policy—told a reporter: "Thinking ahead and having creative solutions for when there is a downturn is what management is all about."[22]

LIMITING THE SOCIAL COSTS IN A TURBULENT LABOR MARKET

Powerful economic forces are driving United States employers—and employers elsewhere across the globe—toward the employability model as the best option among a constrained set of labor arrangements. Social pressure and governmental regulation will be necessary to prevent firms operating in a capitalist global context from restructuring the employment contract in a fashion that promotes the highest (short-term) profits of the company at the expense of reasonable economic security for employees. One important social issue is distributing the social costs incurred when workers are displaced. It is unfair that the costs of restructuring and economic growth be paid by an arbitrarily harmed group—the displaced workers.

Under current conditions in a global economy where capitalism reigns unchallenged, it may be unrealistic to strive for government policies that promote "job security," i.e., a guarantee that a worker can remain in *the same job*. Moreover, rigid job security would stifle economic innovation that benefits many people, including many workers. It would be more realistic to focus on policies that allow workers to move among jobs without suffering serious losses of income or benefits.[23]

There are government policies that could cushion the economic shocks felt by displaced workers. One important step in the right direction was recently enacted legislation called the Health Insurance Portability and Accountability Act of 1996 (the Kassebaum-Kennedy Bill). This legislation prohibited insurance companies from refusing to cover "pre-existing [medical] conditions" when a new employee was added to a company's policy. This removed the threat that a worker would lose crucial insurance coverage for serious ongoing medical problems when changing jobs. Disturbingly, however, the General Accounting Office of the federal government reports that this health insurance legislation has not been effective in many instances. Many insurance companies are only offering coverage at prohibitively high prices; some companies are actively discouraging insurance agents from selling policies to eligible individuals.[24]

An important proposal being discussed today is legislation to encourage pension "portability." A system could be devised to allow displaced workers to transfer the moneys that they and their employers have contributed to a pension plan into a new pension account. Upon retirement, the employee would draw benefits based on this broad base of pension contributions. The TIAA-CREF plan, which provides pension portability for employees of institutions of higher education, is an example of such a system.

In the advanced welfare states of Europe, it is possible to imagine that government policies would encourage the provision of a basic salary and benefits package that would be similar across employers and industries, so that workers who lost one job could expect to receive similar rewards if they found a new job elsewhere. In the European context, Werner Sengenberger could seriously suggest "the standardization of the terms of employment between firms or establishments, with regard to wages, fringe benefits, and working conditions."[25] In making this suggestion, Sengenberger had in mind particularly the "solidaristic wage" policy in Sweden in which wages and benefits for certain categories of jobs "were balanced according to region, skill, industry, and gender."[26] If the rewards of jobs were so standardized, then a worker who lost a job in a downsizing firm or a declining industry could expect to receive similar wages and benefits in a new position. The personal and familial losses associated with job loss would be substantially mitigated. However, the social and political climate makes such a proposal unrealistically "utopian" in the current United States context.

There are other forms of governmental intervention that might be politically feasible in the United States. Under United States tax law, investors already get tax deductions for capital losses when monetary investments go sour. What about tax credits related to the loss of "human capital" suffered by workers who lose job tenure? Former Secretary of Labor Robert Reich has suggested that an employee who loses one job and who suffers a wage loss when taking a new job should be offered a wage subsidy equal to one-half the difference between the (higher) old salary and the (lower) new wage. The subsidy would be for one year to give displaced workers and their families time to make a financial transition.[27]

In the shift toward an employability contract, there is more burden on individuals to attain and upgrade "employability." In its 1997 economic report, the Clinton administration suggests consolidating a variety of federal job retraining programs—a unified voucher program that would subsidize skills training for displaced workers. The government could also establish tax policies that encourage individuals to invest in their own human capital or could allow people to establish tax-free savings accounts to be used for skills training expenses. Alternatively, legislators could permit tax deductions or tax credits for employment training expenses. Unfortunately, education savings accounts, tax deductions, and tax credits would benefit moderate- to high-income workers who have extra income for savings and who pay enough taxes to benefit from tax deductions or credits. The lowest-income workers would not benefit from such tax plans. These workers might benefit more from a plan under which the government and employers cooperated in offering training to employees whose present jobs were being eliminated. Paul Loseby suggests that employees who are about to be laid off could be given "the alternative of remaining on the payroll and being paid the equivalent of unemployment benefits while taking part in education and training programs approved by the employer."[28]

There are, of course, problems with these proposals. Most importantly, under global capitalism, financial capital may move to those nations that do the least to protect workers who lose jobs in a dynamic economy. Policies protecting the interests of workers would be highly vulnerable to business complaints that higher labor costs were undermining national economic competitiveness. Policies to protect displaced workers might rebound against such workers unless the economy was simultaneously creating new jobs at a steady clip. Otherwise, policies promoting economic security for workers might trap some more or less permanently outside the labor force. Conservative commentators make this point when they examine the stubbornly high unemployment rates in European countries that provide much greater employment security to workers. Policies to protect displaced workers would only be politically feasible if there were international labor and regulatory institutions that could promote the well-being of workers simultaneously in many nations.

3

THE GROWTH OF CONTINGENT WORK

A disturbing number of jobs in the United States labor force are jobs that are explicitly designed to be short-term, that is, contingent jobs. Since the 1980s, various forms of contingent employment have been growing rapidly throughout the world. While more full-time, long-term jobs were finally created well into the economic expansion of the 1990s, the underlying trend seems to be one of less permanence in employment relationships. While employers and some workers value the "flexibility" inherent in contingent employment relationships, some of these jobs have a number of morally problematic aspects. Economist Robert Kuttner cautions: "Part-time and temp work is the fastest growing sector of the great American jobs machine and *the underside* of today's boom."[1]

Ethicists who are concerned about economic issues need to take a closer look at the darker underside. In some major corporations, a significant minority of the workers going in the door on any given day are not on the permanent payroll. In addition, a noteworthy number of persons doing work for the corporations are doing it on a subcontract basis at other locations. Indeed, the management literature is full of advice that companies should distinguish between core employees who have skills and knowledge critical to the success of the business and others whose function is less crucial.[2] The performance of the so-called peripheral functions can be subcontracted—"outsourced"—or performed by expendable contingent workers. When labor costs need to be trimmed, the core workforce is protected; subcontracts are cut back or eliminated; and contingent workers are shed.[3]

Some observers report a growth in a human resources strategy that they call "planned staffing." This means that management determines a firm's crucial activities and the number of employees necessary to staff those crucial functions during a lean period. That limited number of employees is the permanent workforce whose employment is relatively secure. Then the firm uses a variety of contingent arrangements to respond to increased demand during periods of economic expansion. One major way to increase staff during an upturn without ongoing commitment to the workers is to hire temporary workers. For example, a firm may have a basic nucleus of permanent employees adequate to staff a shipping department during a period of limited sales. If sales expand, temporary laborers are added only as long as demand remains high. Robert Parker states that "planning staffing is a particularly critical development . . . because it encourages a growing . . . use of temporary workers."[4]

HOW MANY CONTINGENT WORKERS?

There are differing definitions of contingent work and differing estimates about the size of the contingent workforce. The most detailed information on contingent work comes from a special survey that the United States Bureau of Labor Statistics conducted in conjunction with the Current Population Survey (CPS) in February 1995.[5] This survey was designed to highlight the ephemeral nature of contingent jobs. Thus the survey focused on workers who told data collectors that their jobs were not expected to continue. In this study, contingent jobs are "jobs which are structured to last only a limited period of time."[6] The researchers focused on "individuals who do not perceive themselves as having an explicit or implicit contract for ongoing employment." This is the most restrictive definition of contingent work. Thus, this survey was designed by researchers who had previously focused on "the low degree of *job security*" in contingent employment. They considered the most salient aspect of contingent jobs to be their configuration as "'on-demand' employment."[7] Using this narrow definition of contingent work, 5 percent of the workers surveyed by the Bureau of Labor Statistics said their jobs were "temporary or not expected to continue." At 5 percent, six million workers are in jobs that they know will not continue.

In the February 1995 CPS supplement on contingent work, the designers also collected data on what they called "alternative employment arrangements." These alternative labor arrangements included independent contractors, "on call" workers, persons working for temporary help services agencies, and people working for business services firms that "provided the worker's services to one customer at that customer's worksite."[8] One in ten United States workers worked in an alternate employment arrangement.[9] However, in the Bureau of Labor Statistics study, many of these workers were not added to the contingent labor estimates because they did not state that their jobs had only a short-term future.

A noted expert on contingent labor, Richard Belous, uses a broader definition of contingent work. While he described contingent workers as "workers who do not have a long-term attachment to their employers," Belous actually focused on a large group of workers who did not have *full-time* jobs with long-range employment prospects. Using this broad definition, Belous's most cautious estimate was that 24 percent of United States workers were in contingent jobs in the late 1980s. Moreover, contingent work was growing rapidly. According to Belous, during the 1980s, at least 33 percent of the new jobs created were contingent jobs.[10]

However, Belous made several debatable judgments in analyzing contingent work. First, he made a questionable judgment when he included all "business services" employees in his less cautious estimates. Business services employees are a large, growing, and diverse group. This category includes employees of major advertising and management consulting firms who have full-time jobs with good benefits; these jobs have a long horizon for employment. Other business services workers are employees of companies like private security firms. Such workers receive lower wages and fewer benefits and often have a higher turnover. The lower-level workers in some business services firms share many of the employment risks that are associated with contingent work. Other employees, particularly in business services companies providing professional expertise or managerial advice, do not face those employment disadvantages.[11] In fact, in the 1995 supplement to the CPS, government researchers found that only 12.8 percent of business services workers were in jobs that the workers expected not to continue. (However, that is still two and one-half times the 4.9 percent rate for the overall labor force.)

The most questionable aspect of Belous's analysis was his decision to include all part-time workers in his estimates of the size and growth of the contingent workforce. Part-time workers, as we shall see in greater detail below, often lack standard fringe benefits and may have less opportunity for job advancement. In many cases, however, they do have long-term job prospects with their current employer. The February 1995 supplement to the CPS, for example, reports that 90 percent of part-time workers expected their jobs to continue for more than one year. If job security is a major concern, then including all part-time workers in estimates of the contingent workforce is a dubious choice.

I have been impressed with the estimate of contingent workers offered by David Gordon. He used the Bureau of Labor Statistics data on contingent workers (strictly defined) to which Gordon adds data on *involuntary* part-time workers, and those in "alternative employment" arrangements who say they would prefer full-time, long-term jobs. Among those in alternative employment relationships whom Gordon considered were independent contractors, day laborers, "temps," and on-call workers who would like to find regular jobs. Gordon found that more than 9 million workers or "roughly a tenth of the private nonfarm wage-and-salary workforce were in 'disposable' employment situations in [February] 1995."[12] Gordon made a persuasive case that in 1995—a year of solid economic growth, a time when there had been a protracted economic expansion—almost one in ten United States workers could reasonably be considered contingent workers. These were workers who experienced unwelcome flexibility in the number of hours of work available to them and/or in the level of employment security available to them.

INVOLUNTARY PART-TIME WORK

Those, such as Nardone and Polivka, who criticize the inclusion of all part-time workers in the category of "contingent workers" have a valid point. There certainly are many part-time workers who have long-term employment relationships and job security in part-time positions. However, there are several differences between part-time and full-time work that are morally troubling. The one that I will focus on in this section is the growth in *involuntary* part-time employment.

In December of 1997, about 17 percent of the labor force was classified as part-time workers. There are actually more part-time jobs than these statistics suggest, because the United States Bureau of Labor Statistics counts the number of workers who work fewer than thirty-five hours per week, not the number of jobs that offer fewer than thirty-five hours of work per week. Some workers who work more than one part-time job in a week and whose total work time exceeds thirty-five hours do not show up as part-time workers, but their jobs are part-time jobs. According to an analysis of 1995 data, almost a million workers "combined several part-time jobs to make up a full-time workweek."[13] According to the same study, women made up 65 percent of those who combined several part-time jobs for a total of thirty-five hours per week or more.

Part-time work has been growing steadily since the 1950s. What is new in recent decades is the rapid growth in involuntary part-time employment. "Between the 1950s and the early 1970s, only voluntary part-time employment outgrew the workforce as a whole, while involuntary part-time work simply kept pace with workforce growth. Beginning in the early 1970s, these positions were reversed, and the ranks of involuntary part-timers swelled faster than overall workforce expansion."[14]

The rate of involuntary part-time employment tends to fluctuate over the business cycle. Involuntary part-time employment rises during recessions, when some employers cut some workers' hours below thirty-five per week because demand for the product or service the workers produce has declined. In addition, during a recession, job seekers who prefer full-time work may find fewer full-time jobs available and, hence, may reluctantly accept part-time positions.

However, in addition to the tendency of involuntary part-time work to increase during a recessionary period, there has been an underlying trend toward an increase in the rate of involuntary part-time employment across the business cycle—in good economic times and in bad. This underlying trend in the proportion of all part-time workers who would prefer to have a full-time position has been on the upswing since 1969.[15] During the 1980s, involuntary part-time work grew rapidly. Indeed, "involuntary part-time work [represented] the fastest-growing employment arrangement during the 1980s. Between 1979 and 1987, it increased about four times as fast as full-time or voluntary part-time employment."[16]

Until the 1990s, involuntary part-time jobs declined during periods of economic expansion. In the early stages of the recovery from the recession of 1990–91, that pattern changed. As late as 1993, Tilly noted: "Furthermore, in the current 'jobless recovery,' involuntary part-time employment actually grew as the economy expanded—the only time this has happened in the post–World War II period."[17] In 1997, Robert Kuttner reported that "about 7 million Americans—roughly a third of all part timers—are working part-time involuntarily."[18]

In addition to the extent of involuntary part-time employment just discussed, many commentators believe that there is a significant amount of disguised involuntary unemployment among women. Some women workers who would like to work longer hours cannot find or afford quality child care, so they restrict their work hours in order to give more attention to their children. These women are classified as voluntary part-time workers, but their choice of working fewer hours has been constrained by poor child care options. In 1994, for the first time, the Bureau of Labor Statistics asked a question designed to elicit information about women in this situation. These government researchers found that 850,000 people who were classified as voluntary part-time workers worked shorter hours "because they had problems arranging child care."[19]

In fact, women are overrepresented in both the voluntary and the involuntary segments of the part-time labor force. Men are clustered among those involuntary part-time workers who usually work full-time but in certain weeks get fewer hours of employment. Construction work is a good example of a field in which male workers sometimes find themselves involuntarily scheduled less than thirty-five hours in a given week. Men aged twenty-five to fifty-four are less likely to work part-time involuntarily than are women in that age group. Still, involuntary part-time work is on the increase even among these prime-age men.[20] Men's overall participation in the part-time labor force more than doubled in the period from 1969 to 1993.[21]

"Minority workers" are overrepresented in the *involuntary* labor force, but not in the voluntary labor force.[22] Both men and women from African American and Hispanic groups have long been disproportionately trapped in part-time positions.[23] The Bureau of Labor Statistics reports: "Both black and Hispanic women who worked part-time were much more likely than white women to do so involuntarily."[24] Workers with less than a high-school education are disproportionately likely to be trapped in involuntary part-time jobs. Labor statistician Thomas Nardone suggests that "their inability to get as much work as they desire may be due to a lack of skills, rather than simply a lack of full-time jobs."[25]

THE TWO FACES OF PART-TIME WORK

While many workers are trapped in involuntary part-time jobs, other workers are quite happy with part-time employment. Economist Chris Tilly has shown that workers can have very different experiences while working part-time. Typical part-time jobs have a number of limitations and drawbacks; what Tilly calls "retention" part-time work offers more positive features for workers. Tilly indicates that retention part-time jobs are a small segment of total part-time employment.[26]

The typical part-time job is structured by the employer as an offer of employment with hours below the "standard work week." In the United States, the standard work week is thirty-five hours or more. Employers often use many part-time workers to supplement staff during limited periods of high demand, such as additional evening hours at a retail store or the limited period of peak sorting activity at a package delivery operation. Staffing shorter periods of peak demand with part-time workers keeps labor costs low. Part-time workers in such ordinary part-time jobs perform routine duties. Their total hours or work schedules may change unpredictably. Ordinary part-time workers may have limited access to company-sponsored training and little opportunity for promotion.

However, other part-time jobs have a far more desirable profile. Tilly has called such jobs "retention" part-time jobs, because he observed that employers often agree to such part-time arrangements in order to retain particular employees who have highly valuable job skills. These valuable employees are unwilling to continue working a full-time schedule. Retention part-timers are usually professional or technical employees.[27] They are more frequently women. These women often negotiate a part-time arrangement in order to balance work with family caretaking activities. Retention part-time workers generally appreciate their employer's willingness to accommodate the employee's preferred schedule. Therefore, they are likely to have a mutually agreeable, long tenure with their employer.

Retention part-timers may already have moved up several steps on a job ladder while they were full-time employees. The skills that had previously won some retention part-timers promotions are the skills that make the employer willing to negotiate a part-time arrangement. However, even retention part-time workers frequently find that their bosses are less likely to consider them for further promotions while they are on a part-time schedule. However, if a retention part-time worker indicates that she is ready to resume full-time work, she may regain her position on a relatively long professional or managerial job ladder.[28]

TEMPORARY WORKERS

The explosive growth of the temporary sector of the workforce over the last twenty-five years is perhaps the best symbol of today's disposable worker. According to *USA Today,* "on an average day in 1990, 1.2 million people were working temporary jobs. [By 1997] the ranks of the temp workers [had] swelled to more than 2.2 million."[29] The largest employer in the United States is no longer General Motors. It is Manpower, Inc., a *multinational* organization with placement agencies throughout the world.

For almost three decades, the temporary help services industry has been booming. Robert Parker quotes a source who indicates that during the late 1970s and early 1980s the temporary help services industry grew "nearly twice as fast as GNP" and grew "faster than the highly touted computer industry (7.9% vs. 6.2% during 1970–83)."[30] That growth accelerated even more during the late 1980s and the 1990s. "Between 1982 and 1993, temporary employment increased 250 percent, ten times faster than the rate of overall employment."[31] Temporary agencies have doubled their business since 1990.

Of particular significance is the growth of the temporary work force throughout the 1990s. In the early years of this present economic expansion, temporary employment accounted for an especially high percentage of all new jobs created. In 1992, 26 percent of net new jobs were temporary positions; in 1993, 15 percent of such jobs were temporary ones.[32] However, economic specialists do point out that since the temporary help services industry is a large industrial sector and since temporary jobs have a relatively short duration, it is predictable that temporary jobs will represent a significant share of all new jobs created.[33]

Chris Tilly points out a new phenomenon in the mid-1990s that may indicate that organizations are becoming more committed to a human resources strategy that includes a significant reliance on temporary workers. Tilly says, "While firms have traditionally taken on temps early in an economic expansion but replaced them with permanent employees as economic growth takes off, during the most recent recovery [1991–] businesses bucked tradition by continuing to add temporary employees."[34]

Thus, Tilly draws our attention to a cyclical pattern in the use of temporary workers, but a pattern that is being modified as firms continue to use temporaries more heavily throughout the 1990s. The statistics on temporary jobs are similar to the statistics on involuntary part-time work. The levels of each type of employment fluctuate over the business cycle. When the economy is in a period of prolonged economic growth, temporary work, like involuntary part-time work, declines. Employers are confident about business prospects and willing to provide full-time, permanent jobs for a larger group of workers. The labor market is relatively tight, so potential workers who want full-time, permanent jobs can hold out for the kind of job offer that they prefer. Despite the fluctuations in temporary work over the business cycle, the underlying trend is growth in temporary employment as a share of all employment.[35]

Companies are now using temporary workers on a long-term basis while avoiding a direct employment relationship with these workers. The Bureau of Labor Statistics found in 1995 that 16 percent of temporary help agency workers "had been working at their current assignment for more than a year."[36] One early study found that the largest companies were increasing their use of temporaries the most. On the basis of that study, Callaghan and Hartmann warn: "The THS [Temporary Help Supply] industry . . . facilitates the development of more casual systems of labor relations in the sectors of the labor market that once provided the greatest degree of job security."[37]

The largest number of temporary workers are performing clerical tasks. Industrial worker positions also account for many temporary assignments. However, there has been steady growth in the

professional segment of the temporary help services industry. Some
of this growth in temporary work for professionals is due to the
restructuring of the health care industry. Hospitals and other
health care providers are using more temporary workers in professional positions, such as nursing positions. A reporter for *The
New York Times,* reviewing investment opportunities in temporary help services companies, writes: "And as a growing number
of specialty staffing companies focus on farming out high-end professionals, they can reap something else that Wall Street has not
seen recently from the industry: high operating margins, often 50
percent higher than those of traditional temporary-help firms."[38]

Much of the data on the use of temporary workers is based on
workers provided by temporary help companies. However, information suggests that a growing number of corporations are hiring
workers for temporary positions themselves without going
through a temporary help services firm. Robert Parker reports,
"Using in-house temps or direct hires on a temporary basis has become a central component in the reorganized staffing patterns of
many private enterprises, including Control Data Corporation,
Travelers Insurance, and Cigna Insurance. Public-sector employers
such as educational institutions as well as nonprofit organizations,
frequently use in-house temporary workers."[39] Polly Callaghan
and Heidi Hartmann say that there may be as many workers on
temporary assignments hired directly by companies as workers
hired through temporary help services firms.[40] Françoise Carré indicates that scanty evidence suggests that the number of temporary
workers hired directly by the employers "far surpasses the size of
employment in the THS [temporary help services] industry."[41]

In some cases, a large corporation may have enough fluctua-
tion in staffing demands to give some employees in the in-house
"temporary" pool full-time work opportunities. These employees
have stable jobs as "floaters" who are assigned to a variety of de-
partments that need labor on a temporary basis. John Sweeney and
Karen Nussbaum cite Federal Express as a company that provides
permanent employment for a group of employees who rotate
through a series of assignments as the company's staffing needs
fluctuate.[42] In many other cases, however, companies hire workers
directly for short-term assignments with no commitment to providing ongoing work opportunities.

DISPLACED WORKERS BECOME DISPOSABLE WORKERS

There is limited evidence to suggest that workers who were looking for new jobs in the mid-1990s were somewhat more likely to be shunted into contingent jobs. Data collected in February 1995 showed that almost 9 percent of workers who had been in their present positions for three years or less were working in contingent positions. That was almost twice the rate of contingent employment as that for the workforce as a whole. In addition, it was not only the youngest workers in new jobs who were disproportionately filling contingent jobs. Workers over twenty-five who had taken a job within the last three years had double the rate of contingent employment as well.[43]

In one ironic twist, 55 percent of firms that had eliminated jobs in 1995–96 reported to American Management Association researchers that they had increased their use of contingent and temporary workers.[44] Some of those contingent workers might even have been former employees who, after being downsized, were offered assignments on a short-term basis. Louis Uchitelle has reported that preliminary data shows that almost one-fifth of contract workers performing duties for United States businesses are actually former employees of those companies who are brought back on a contingent basis after leaving the company payroll. An American Management Association study found that 30 percent of companies that had recently been through a period of downsizing subsequently hired former employees on a temporary or contract basis. Economist Alan Krueger told Uchitelle that bringing former employees back on a contract worker basis is a way for corporations to benefit from former workers' specialized expertise without incurring fixed labor costs. Krueger continued: "And that is an important step that companies are taking toward rewriting the implicit contract that bound them to their workers."[45]

Henry Farber's analysis of government data shows displaced workers looking for new positions are being channeled in greater numbers into part-time positions. He reports: "The striking fact is that while about 11 percent of displaced workers were displaced from part-time jobs, fully 25 percent of displaced workers employed at the survey date are employed in part-time jobs. Thus, an obvious important consequence of job loss is the inability to find a new full-time job."[46] Farber found that it was particularly workers who had lost their jobs because of "slack work" who had to settle for part-time work after they lost a full-time position. Since blue-collar workers, including many minority workers and/or workers with less education, were more likely to lose their jobs due to "slack work," those workers would have been shunted into part-time positions. Displaced workers suffered serious financial loss related to their job loss, in part because a significant minority of displaced workers could only find work in part-time positions.[47]

Contingent work is on the rise across the globe. Part-time work, temporary work, and independent contract assignments represent rapidly growing forms of labor in Italy, Spain, Norway, the United Kingdom, Germany, and Japan.[48] Guy Standing reports: "There is a global trend to reduced reliance on full-time wage and salary workers earning fixed wages and various fringe benefits. Companies and public sector enterprises in both developed and developing economies are increasingly resorting to casual or temporary workers, to part-timers, to subcontracting and to contract workers. In the process, they further erode employment and income security."[49]

SOCIAL PROBLEMS ASSOCIATED WITH CONTINGENT LABOR

Some workers welcome contingent work arrangements. Part-time work offers many workers, especially retention part-time workers, more time to devote to other activities that they value highly such as education or family life. Some contract workers, particularly some professionals and managers, like the flexibility and the constant challenges that work with a variety of clients brings. Still there are a number of social issues associated with a global drive toward increasingly contingent work relations. I will review nine disturbing features of contingent work.

First, workers who cannot get standard, full-time jobs often have to settle for lower wages and fewer fringe benefits. Indeed, in the United States, many employers use contingent labor *because they can avoid offering costly fringe benefits*. Françoise Carré reports on one large study that found that the better (and more expensive) a company's benefits package for its regular workers, the more likely the company was to use temporary workers who had no claim to those generous benefits.[50]

Temporary workers earn lower hourly wages than their counterparts in permanent positions. In 1990, the average hourly wage for temporary workers was $7.73 compared to $10.03 for permanent workers. This hourly wage ratio has "remained stable over time."[51] One reason that temporary workers get lower wages is that the pay for a temporary worker is usually pegged to the entry-level wage for the position that they are filling.[52] Low total wages may be a special problem for African American temporary workers, because African Americans are disproportionately likely to work fewer than thirty-five hours a week on their temporary assignments.[53]

Male workers suffer a greater loss of earnings when working as temporary workers. There are two reasons for this. First, the industrial jobs that men staff as temps are more likely to be part-time; the clerical jobs that women staff are more likely to be full-time. Second, there is a greater gap between the lower wages of temporary industrial workers and the wages of their counterparts in permanent industrial positions. There is a smaller gap between the wages paid to temporary and permanent workers in the predominantly female clerical field.[54]

Anne Polivka and Thomas Nardone indicate that "fewer than one-quarter of temporary help employees work in [THS] firms that offer health benefits."[55] A survey of temps working for Manpower, the world's largest temporary help services business, found that few of its workers received health care coverage from Manpower's plan.[56] Just because a firm offers health insurance benefits does not mean that many of the temporary workers actually qualify to participate in the plan. In a number of cases, health insurance coverage is available only to those workers who amass a substantial number of hours working for the temporary help agency. Many workers find it difficult to get assignments steadily enough to meet the hourly requirements for participation in the health plan. In addition, some temporary agencies that provide health insurance only offer a chance for the temp to sign up with the agency's group policy, but the agency does not offer to pay the premium as a fringe benefit. In a number of cases, even the few temporary workers who qualify for health insurance coverage must elect to pay the entire premium cost themselves.[57]

The situation is even bleaker when pension plans are considered. Only 2 percent of temporary help agencies offer pension plans. The nature of temporary work is such that it is almost impossible for temporary workers to work steadily enough to build up credits in a conventional pension system. In one related situation, Travelers Insurance company had a highly publicized program in which they hired their own retirees as an in-house temporary workforce. However, it was the company's policy to keep the total hours of any retiree "at or below 960 hours per year to prevent them from accruing additional pension credits that would increase their pension income."[58]

Part-time workers face similar problems. Part-time work often pays a lower rate per hour than the rate for comparable full-time positions. Studies have shown that even when factors such as age, educational level, and job classification are held constant, part-time workers earn about 17 to 30 percent less per hour than full-time workers.[59] David Gordon found that those who were working part-time *involuntarily* "earned almost a quarter less than full-time workers with comparable characteristics."[60] Rebecca Blank indicates that women working part-time involuntarily suffer increased wage penalties.[61]

However, part-time workers in technical and professional fields are more likely to receive hourly wages comparable to those of full-time workers. Indeed, women in part-time managerial and professional positions sometimes earn *more* per hour than their full-time counterparts.[62] Male professionals also get a favorable part-time wage rate.[63]

While professionals may be able to command relatively high part-time wages, most part-time workers suffer serious financial disadvantages. The combination of reduced hours and lower rates of pay per hour results in low income for many part-time workers. Chris Tilly reports: "Part-timers . . . are a growing group with low hourly wages and *very* low annual wages."[64] Indeed, Tilly concludes that more than 40 percent of the growth of wage inequality during the period 1978 to 1984 "could be accounted for by the growth of part-time employment" and the growing gap between the earnings of part-time and full-time workers.[65]

Many part-time workers receive limited fringe benefits. Part-time workers are much less likely to be covered by health insurance provided by their employers. Many commentators point out that the majority of part-time workers in the United States are married women, who may have health insurance coverage provided through their husbands' jobs. A number of young part-time workers may be covered by their parents' health care policies. Older part-time workers may have Medicare coverage. However, studies show that there are a significant number of part-time workers who have no health insurance coverage at all. Tilly cites surveys that show that 21 percent of part-time workers (compared to 16 percent of full-time workers) have no health insurance "from any source, including [the] government." Among workers working part-time involuntarily, "almost one-third" had no health insurance coverage.[66]

Part-time workers are even less likely to have pension coverage that will provide an income in old age. This is because part-time workers are less likely to be covered by a pension plan. Additionally, they are less likely to meet the "vesting" requirements in order to qualify for pension payments from the plans in which they do participate. Studies show that only 11 to 20 percent of part-time workers receive pension coverage from their employers.[67] Even fewer part-time workers actually qualify to draw pension benefits.[68] Involuntary part-time workers are less likely to participate in an employer-sponsored pension plan than are voluntary part-time workers. Men working part-time involuntarily are even less likely to be covered by a pension plan than women in that situation.[69]

A second social problem is that women are overrepresented among contingent workers. Part-time work and temporary work are types of contingent labor in which women predominate. This is true across the industrialized world. Two Australian commentators talk about "an expanding peripheral workforce—mostly women—part-time, casual, short-term contract and temporary workers."[70]

There is a fit between gender ideology and contingent work as women's work. Women workers are still seen as more likely to have major domestic duties. Many people expect that a woman's family responsibilities will take precedence over her workplace commitments. The same people also frequently expect that a woman's wages will make a secondary contribution to the financial resources of a family. The assumption is that each woman has a husband who, as the breadwinner, assumes the lion's share of the financial responsibility in the family. As long as this schema of husband/breadwinner and wife/family caretaker holds true, then it is not a serious problem if a woman's job provides a lower wage or fewer benefits. After all, the family can rely on the salary and benefits from the husband's [standard] job.

Sociologist Kevin Henson argues that an ideology of women as primarily homemakers making only a secondary financial contribution to the family was a key to the structuring of temporary work. He says:

> Early temporary agencies assumed from the beginning that temporary employment was "women's work." This assumption was reflected in the common inclusion of the word "girl" in the names of the newly formed temporary agencies (such as Kelly Girl, Western Girl, Right Girl). Recruitment efforts in the early industry specifically targeted and courted women. Women who worked as temporaries, however, were reminded that their participation should always be secondary to their primary feminine roles as wives and mothers. Temporary employment, with its intermittent work availability and without a promotional track, fit well with an existing national ideology that assumed that women's labor was transitory, impermanent, and secondary.[71]

Thus, gender stereotypes have historically been used to justify women's exploitation as a source of contingent labor. Women's participation in the contingent labor force continues across the globe today.

Women's disproportionate presence in the contingent labor force is contributing to serious economic inequalities between men and women in later life. In particular, the lack of pension coverage associated with many contingent labor arrangements contributes to a serious situation for older women. In the United States, almost 60 percent of women employed in the private sector are not covered by a pension plan. More than half of retired male workers receive pension benefits other than Social Security payments. Less than one-third of female workers receive such benefits. Women's greater participation in temporary and part-time work means that they have less money to live on when they retire.[72]

Third, persons from racial and ethnic minority groups are also overrepresented in contingent jobs. African Americans are twice as likely to work in temporary positions as their overall share in the labor force would indicate.[73] This is true, in part, because African American men are disproportionately likely to fill temporary laborer positions. African American women are also overrepresented in temporary clerical positions. Callaghan and Hartmann say:

> The disproportionate representation in contingent work of groups that typically experience discrimination in the labor market suggests that for most workers contingent work is a last resort rather than a first choice. The limited opportunities for decent wages and benefits and the make-up of the contingent workforce suggest that the progress brought about by affirmative action, pay equity, and other equal opportunity programs is likely to be eroded as contingent work continues to grow.[74]

Throughout the world, immigrants and people from socially disadvantaged ethnic groups are found disproportionately in low-paying, contingent positions.

Fourth, the contingent workforce may receive less employer-provided training in work skills. Employers have less incentive to pay for training for workers whose jobs with the company have a short horizon. In addition, part-time or temporary workers may not have the money to invest in enhancing their own skills.[75]

There may be a painful rebound resulting from low investment in training for contingent workers. Callaghan and Hartmann warn "if such . . . staffing patterns prevent the training and investment in workers that is needed to make a better long-run adaptation to changing employment requirements, the short-cut of using contingent workers may be reducing, rather than increasing, productivity growth over the long run."[76] And increasing productivity is the key to meeting increased human needs and using environmental resources more efficiently and, hence, more responsibly.

Fifth, many contingent workers are not covered by protective labor legislation. Contract workers and temps are *not employees* of the client firm, so they do not have the legal protections afforded employees. Since they are not covered by the Family and Medical Leave Act, they are not guaranteed leaves in the event of the sickness of a family member, for example. Since such contingent workers are not employees, they are not counted when a firm develops an equal opportunity employment and promotion profile. If the temps who filled clerical positions or the professionals working on a contract basis are disproportionately European

American, for example, this would not be reflected in an evaluation of the firm's affirmative action efforts.[77]

The reduced legal rights of contingent workers are a problem in other nations, too. Scandinavian researchers point out that workers laboring under contingent work arrangements do not receive the protections accorded workers in standard work relationships. For example, in Sweden a parent who is working as a temporary is not entitled to the generous parental leave mandated for regular employees, male or female.[78]

On the other hand, certain government social policies can have as an unintended consequence the promotion of contingent work relationships. The much more elaborate government regulations concerning the termination of workers in certain European countries have been an important factor in the rapid growth of contingent work arrangements in those nations.

Sixth, for some workers, a pattern is emerging that Swedish researchers call "permanent temporariness." In a thought-provoking Swedish study, female workers and workers with less education depended on a series of temporary jobs after their long-term manufacturing jobs were eliminated. Male and better-educated workers had more success in finding secure employment within two years.[79] While this study was carried out in Sweden, we need to find out whether some significant groups of American workers also find themselves in a situation of "permanent temporariness."

There is a hint that such a pattern might be emerging for some United States workers in data from the Bureau of Labor Statistics. Workers in contingent positions (strictly defined) were much more likely to report that their last job was a temporary job that they lost because it ended. Almost 24 percent of contingent workers described that as the situation on their last job, compared with only 9 percent of workers overall.[80] In addition, "more than 50 percent of contingent workers had less than one year of tenure in their previous jobs."[81] Polivka, who was concerned whether workers were being terminated from permanent positions and forced to take contingent ones, concluded that it was more likely that contingent workers were "moving from one contingent job to another," rather than moving from permanent jobs to contingent ones.[82]

Françoise Carré describes another kind of permanent temporariness—workers who want permanent jobs but are stuck in temporary jobs for long periods of time. Some temporary workers find that client firms (contracting with temporary help agencies) want their services for relatively long periods of time, but on an insecure, "temporary" basis. Carré reports an increasing number of temporary workers find themselves working on a "temporary" basis for an extensive period for the same corporate client.[83]

Given this evidence that permanent temporariness is a global phenomenon, we need to ask how do gender, racial/ethnic origin, and class influence the likelihood that one will be consigned to a long-term "temporary" status?

Seventh, contingent work is being embraced by employers especially because it gives management substantially enhanced flexibility in their deployment of labor. However, we need to look more closely at what labor expert Guy Standing has labeled "subordinated flexibility."[84] Many contingent workers need work badly. Their bargaining power with employers is limited; and, therefore, flexibility is defined on the employer's terms.

Part-time work gives an employer a variety of types of flexibility. These include: "the ability to increase employee hours without paying overtime or decrease hours without violating a commitment; the ability to cover peak hours; the ability to cover odd shifts such as evenings, nights, and weekends; and access to a pool of workers who can be used to fill in gaps or be moved from one time to another."[85]

So far, I have argued that contingent work provides flexibility primarily on the employer's terms. Now, I want to acknowledge that economic pressures can push particular companies to use contingent work patterns, when that choice might not be consistent with the company's corporate values. Chris Tilly gives a revealing example. At the time Tilly was doing his research on part-time work in the insurance industry, part-time work was relatively rare in that industry. However, some companies were redesigning routine clerical jobs so that they could be done on a part-time (and, hence, lower-cost) basis. An executive at one company told Tilly that his company would not follow this growing industry trend because exploitative part-time positions violated the company's value system. He criticized competitors for exploiting housewives with limited economic options, offering them part-time evening work processing claims. This executive declared: "It's a different philos-

ophy of how you treat employees and it's driven by economic realities, and I suppose if things got tough enough it could come to . . .
[our company], but I don't think it will. . . . There are lots of ways
to skimp, and those ways [are] inconsistent with our philosophy
and culture and approach."[86] Tilly reports that, a few months later,
the company in question dropped its line of health care insurance
products because it could not compete effectively with firms that
lowered their labor costs through forms of contingent work.

Tilly puts this one example in a systemic, capitalist context
when he observes: "Once a critical mass of employers have expanded secondary part-time employment, the competitive pressures to follow suit are substantial, because such a change can
yield cost advantages even when it means a fall in productivity."[87]
The return to investors is even higher, of course, when labor costs
are lowered without a decrease in productivity. Some managers report, for example, that when a job involves certain repetitive clerical tasks, workers are *more alert and more productive* when
working only four to six hours per day.

Eighth, large-scale contingent work arrangements sometimes
put pressure on noncontingent workers to agree to employers' demands in order to retain employment security. Polivka and
Nardone suggest that "firms may also obtain wage and work rule
concessions from their permanent staff by offering them employment security" (which can clearly no longer be taken for granted
as a characteristic of jobs). A veteran labor reporter at *The New
York Times,* Louis Uchitelle, comments: "The growing use of temporary and contract workers has relieved pressure to grant raises
[to regular employees]."[88]

Research shows, for example, that the lower wages and reduced benefits for part-time workers have an adverse effect on the
wages and benefits for full-time workers in occupations and industries where part-time work is common. If full-time workers are
in an industry where at least one-third of the workers are part-
timers, then the full-time workers are 10 percentage points less
likely to have health insurance than full-time workers in other industries. They are 17 percentage points less likely to have pension
coverage.[89] Economists Polly Callaghan and Heidi Hartmann cite
a study showing that a high percentage of part-time workers in an
industry holds down the wages and benefits available to male, full-

time workers. Callaghan and Hartmann conclude: "Bad jobs may drive out good jobs, causing hardship both for the workers involved and the economy as a whole."[90]

Ninth, when major corporations need to lower labor costs, contingent workers can be shed with few corporate repercussions. If continuing work is not offered to contract workers or if persons who work for temporary agencies are told they are no longer needed, then there are no press releases, no news stories, and no public criticism of the downsizing companies.

UNIONS AND CONTINGENT WORK

Finally, these types of contingent labor arrangements all make it more difficult to maintain viable, powerful unions representing a large percentage of workers. There are problems related to union representation even for part-time workers. This is despite the fact that the majority of part-time workers have reasonably long-term employment relationships with a given employer. My point is that most part-time workers are present in the workplace for a long enough period to be recruited as union members and to benefit from that union representation. However, in countries such as the United States, the United Kingdom, and Canada, part-time workers are much less likely to belong to a union. Moreover, the number of part-timers joining unions "has lagged well behind growth in the part-time work force."[91] In fact, in the United States, the unionization rate for part-time workers is declining.[92]

The relationship between increasing part-time work and decreasing union power may move in another direction as well. As unions become weaker, workers may be less able to resist creation of less desirable part-time positions. Lonnie Golden says: "It is also not surprising that the rise of involuntary part-time employment coincides with a period of declining unionization in the United States. Workers have lost bargaining leverage over decisions regarding work hours and employment."[93]

The National Labor Relations Board has rendered differing decisions about whether part-time workers were eligible to vote in elections to determine whether a workplace would be unionized and, if so, by what union. In some cases, unions have been successful in bargaining for better contracts for part-time workers. Some unions have been able to gain parity in the hourly wage rate and prorated benefits for part-time workers. Some union contracts stipulate that when a full-time position becomes vacant, members of the bargaining unit who are working part-time but would prefer full-time work must have the first opportunity to fill the full-time vacancy.

In the summer of 1997, the heavily publicized Teamsters' strike against United Parcel Service highlighted worker dissatisfaction with part-time positions. Throughout the 1990s, a decade of economic growth for both UPS and the national economy, four out of five new jobs that UPS created were part-time jobs that paid substantially less than full-time positions. Contrary to the prevailing pattern, UPS did provide health insurance benefits for its part-time workers. The Teamsters gained overwhelming public support by emphasizing that a company like UPS that was making high profits should also be creating more full-time jobs for workers who wanted such jobs. As a Teamster spokesperson put it, "UPS wants throwaway jobs that no one can live on. It's time that somebody stood up to them and said: 'This is not the right direction for America. This is not the right direction for our communities and for working families.'"[94] The Teamsters prevailed after a fifteen-day strike, winning an agreement from management to create an additional 20,000 full-time positions over the five-year contract.

Temporary workers and other contingent workers are even more difficult to unionize than part-time workers. Additionally, some workers, such as temps and "leased" employees, have two employment relationships. They are employed by the temporary help services agency or the employee leasing firm, but they are doing the work of the firm that contracts with the temp agency or employee leasing firm according to the "client" firm's instructions and frequently on the client firm's premises. This twofold employment relationship makes it more difficult for workers in these situations to gain some control over the conditions of their labor. Virginia du Rivage indicates that "Taft-Harley's ban on secondary boycotts makes it difficult for leased employees to act collectively to protest the practices of the leasing employer."[95]

Some managers view temporary workers' lack of connections to unions as an advantage. One business journalist spoke positively about "a temporary worker [who] comes in fresh, alert, and ready to work, and is *not socially or politically involved with the other workers."*[96] Indeed, employers can bring in temporary workers to staff facilities where the regular workforce is on strike.[97]

For workers in the most flexible arrangements, some have suggested a vast expansion of what Guy Standing terms "associational unions," that is, groups that provide collective representation by creating an "association" to represent the interests of an aggregate of individual workers, who do not work together in specific workplaces.[98] The idea here is similar to Actors Equity, which represents individual actors, many of whom move frequently from one relatively short-term job to another. Chris Tilly calls attention to unions in the construction trades, where workers also frequently move from one employer to another. Tilly points out that the trade unions in construction have found ways in which "the union, not the firm, provides stability and equity in terms of wages, health benefits, and pensions."[99] Chris Benner also advocates an increase in the number of unions that organize workers, including contingent workers, based on their shared occupations rather than their shared employer and worksite. Benner suggests that such groups could develop a sense of solidarity based on a common occupational commitment. The goal of such unions would be employment security within an occupation for its members, not a guarantee of continuing employment in a specific job or even with a specific employer.[100]

If temporary workers were eligible to join some sort of workers' association, the association could bargain for affordable health insurance coverage. It could offer a portable retirement account plan where workers and temporary help services agencies contributed funds based on wages earned on a variety of client assignments. One possible model is the national collective bargaining agreement that covers temporary workers in France. This agreement allows workers to build up pension credits not only from one temporary assignment to another, but also from their work with multiple temporary help services agencies. The French temporary workers have genuine pension portability.

WHO BENEFITS FROM THE MOST FLEXIBLE JOB ARRANGEMENTS?

Contingent labor arrangements give management more immediate control over labor costs. Many types of contingent labor can be shed relatively quickly. Temporary workers can be dismissed at the end of the day if there is not sufficient work tomorrow to keep the temporary worker busy. The employer has no obligation to provide additional work for a contract worker once the initial contract is fulfilled, and contracts can sometimes be abrogated in the middle of the engagement.

A variety of contingent labor arrangements turn workers from a fixed cost to a variable cost. This gives management an important lever to adjust expenses in pursuit of optimal profits. Richard Belous comments that flexible labor arrangements "may be the most important control mechanism that management has in the short run, given that management often can treat labor as a variable cost while other costs usually are fixed.[101]

Most contingent workers in the United States do not welcome this type of "flexibility." Only one-third of the contingent workers identified in the 1995 CPS supplement said they preferred contingent work. If the responses of contingent workers who were also students were dropped, only about 20 percent of contingent workers preferred contingent work arrangements.

The result of expanding contingent labor arrangements is to transform radically the configuration of moral obligations that corporations and their managers have to persons who are doing the work necessary for the corporation to function effectively. Richard Belous uses interesting language when he describes this transformation in employment patterns as a change in "the stake" that management permits workers to have as a result of the employment relationship. He reports: "Many employers are in the process of shifting the stake workers have in specific establishments. Workers may not be viewed as part of a corporate entity."[102] Contingent workers—with the exception of part-time workers—are not employees, they have become quasi-suppliers.

Robert Parker suggests that temporary work has grown so rapidly in part because it allows corporations to minimize the size of the workforce for which it is held socially accountable. He says, "The ability of employers to flexibly adjust their workforces at will without any accountability for the associated social costs has contributed to the temporary help industry's rapid ascendancy in the U.S. economy."[103] A client that obtains a worker from a temporary agency is not responsible for health care insurance, pension contributions, or unemployment benefits. But the larger society will have to deal with the suffering of workers who are denied access to these goods. Or the common good will be further diminished as the trend toward a core workforce with economic security and a contingent labor pool facing a precarious economic future accelerates.

There is an assumption in business ethics that employees are second only to stockholders as a constituency to which businesses are morally accountable. Under the post–World War II social contract concerning jobs, the long-term relationship between employer and employee and the employees' economic vulnerability within the employment relationship gave rise to important moral obligations on the employer's part. A corporation was understood to have a different, and somewhat lesser, moral responsibility to the corporation's suppliers. An important moral shift takes place—or appears to take place—when contingent workers become quasi-suppliers, not "real" employees. Chris Tilly warns:

> Employers have shifted more responsibility for health-care insurance and adequate wages onto workers themselves. It is this unilateral employer abdication of responsibility that has turned flexibility from a positive into a negative in many cases.[104]

Temporary work and contract labor arrangements take the "employability" contract to the extreme. The company using the contingent worker's labor abrogates all responsibility to provide employment security for the worker. Thus, the worker becomes entirely responsible for his or her economic security and that of his or her dependents. In chapter 5, I will examine moral theories that help us evaluate the moral legitimacy of this shift.

First, however, I want to examine the complex situation of diverse women in today's workplace. While some women in contingent job arrangements do not earn a living wage, other women in full-time professional and managerial jobs are earning good wages. A relatively small but significant group of women who hold good jobs are doing much better than a growing group of men who are losing out in a global, information economy. Thus, a moral assessment of the economic position of women must be carefully nuanced.

4

ECONOMIC INEQUALITIES AND FEMINIST SOLIDARITY

Thirty years into the second wave of the feminist movement, economic changes are taking place that challenge the boundaries of feminist ethics. Economic inequalities have grown in the United States during the same period when there has been renewed attention to women's rights. Some women, primarily white women, find that their own economic successes place them on the privileged side of a large economic divide. Simultaneously, the economic situation of many white men—whom many feminists viewed as unjustly privileged in comparison to women—is increasingly precarious. Economic location now intersects with gender and race in more complicated ways that make questions in feminist ethics more complex than ever before.

Many feminist scholars have given attention to the economic disparities among women. These scholars have paid special attention to the relative situations of white and black women. Measured in terms of the wages for full-time, year-round workers, the economic status of white and black women converged during the early years of the women's liberation movement. Disturbingly, however, a wage gap favoring white women opened again in the 1980s. In addition, women from all racial/ethnic groups who have a college education or postgraduate education reap an increasing bonus for their knowledge-based skills compared with women who have a high school education or less.

Not only are economic gaps growing among women, but a gap is also growing between economically privileged female workers and economically disadvantaged male workers. Women who hold high-paying—primarily professional and managerial—jobs are garnering a larger share of the economy's rewards while certain groups of men are losing considerable ground economically. Moreover, the men on the disadvantaged side of the economic divide are not exclusively racial/ethnic men. Growing groups of white men face worsening economic stresses—in particular, younger men with limited education and men over fifty-five who lose so-called good jobs are suffering serious losses under current economic conditions.

In a more complex economy, solidarity becomes an important moral virtue for economically privileged women. Moreover, the solidarity to which financially successful women are called goes beyond the "solidarity of sex" that the women's movement has championed. Economically privileged women are called to a solidarity that encompasses concern for the well-being of those male workers who are most at risk given the new job contract.

Contemporary Roman Catholic social thought contains important insights about the virtue of solidarity. An examination of Catholic social thought shows how Christian beliefs provide a firm foundation for this moral obligation. The doctrines of creation, redemption, and sanctification, properly understood, provide elements of an answer to the question, "Why am I obligated to care about the plight of those who are less secure and less employable in the knowledge-based economy of the twenty-first century?"

THE ECONOMIC SITUATION OF DIVERSE WOMEN IN THE 1990s

The economic realities confronting women today are complex. The very real progress that many women have made in the labor force does not mean that women have achieved economic equality with men. Nothing should detract from the fact that there is still a lack of gender equality for women—even for women in the most privileged economic strata. Women—predominantly white women—have increased their share of jobs in the professions and in management. However, a more careful look shows that women are clustered in the less powerful, less well-paying management sectors and in the traditionally feminine professions or "the *nonelite*, [formerly] *male* professions."[1]

Even when women enter high-prestige, high-paying professions such as medicine and law, they are often clustered in specialties that command less prestige and pay, such as pediatrics or family law. Female managers and professionals are often hired disproportionately by those employers who offer lower status and lower pay. Female college professors, for example, are more likely to be employed by community colleges and less likely to be employed by the most highly respected "research universities." In a study of the movement of women into a series of formerly male-dominated professional and managerial categories, Barbara Reskin and Patricia Roos state: "The occupational-level desegregation we observed masked a substantial amount of persistent internal segregation"[2] In other words, for example, more women are managers, but they are managers at the lower ranks or in the industries in which managerial pay is relatively low.

Women are less likely to reach the *highest levels* of pay and prestige in management and in many professions. Women are now represented in the general managerial category in numbers proportionate to their share of the labor force as a whole. Yet women are very underrepresented in top executive positions. Women hold 5 percent or less of the most senior executive positions.

While women have not achieved economic equality with men in the workplace, some women *are* making important occupational strides. In the past few decades, a growing group of women have gained positions of relative economic privilege through their own workplace efforts, not just as daughters of well-to-do fathers or wives of affluent husbands. As some women make important economic advances, *the economic disparities among women workers are growing wider.*

Throughout the 1980s and 1990s, commentators have paid careful attention to the declining wage gap between women and men. (A point about which I will say more below.) Less attention has been paid to the fact that, since 1979, a significant pay gap has been growing among groups of women workers. The economic fortunes of women have been polarizing. In the 1990s income inequalities have been growing among women, partly because a growing number of women have finally gained relatively high-paying jobs and even gained promotions in higher-paying fields.

Thus, the polarization among women workers has grown as more women succeed in gaining a stronger foothold in managerial positions. While men still hold most of the managerial positions, in recent years, women have been gaining new jobs in this sector at a rate greater than the male rate of increase. In the two decades from 1974 to 1994, the share of women workers who were managers (of all types) "more than doubled."[3] Between 1988 and 1995, the number of women employed in managerial fields grew by 31 percent; the number of men grew by 14 percent.[4]

Michael Yates reports the surprising finding that, between 1973 and 1991, women in the top 20 percent of wage earners have been "the only group that enjoyed an increased real wage rate."[5] In the early 1990s, wage rates were falling for all women workers, except those with four or more years of college education.[6] According to the President's Council of Economic Advisors, "the wage premium received by college-educated women roughly doubled between 1978 and 1995, from 38 percent to 70 percent."[7] However, between 1989 and 1995, *the real wages of the lowest 60 percent of women workers* actually declined (when adjusted for inflation).[8] As wages continue to rise for the best-paid women, the gap between groups of women grows at an accelerating rate.

Recently the *gap* between those workers receiving the highest pay and those workers with the lowest pay has been *greater for women* than for men.[9] This gap between the most privileged women and the least privileged women grew, in part, because the least privileged women have been losing ground. For young women with a high school education or less, the penalties for lack of education have grown harsher. During the 1980s, the percentage of such women workers who earned $12,000 a year or less for full-time work grew from 19 percent to 28 percent.[10]

Part of the reason the wages of the lowest-paid women in the United States declined throughout the 1980s was the decline in the value of the minimum wage. In inflation-adjusted dollars, the value of the minimum wage peaked in 1968. Congressional increases in the minimum wage rate partially restored its value in the middle to late 1970s. However, the value of the minimum wage dropped almost every year during 1980s. While Congress has authorized increases several times in the 1990s, the value of the minimum wage is still well below its purchasing power three decades earlier.

For adult workers, the minimum wage is predominantly a woman's wage. In the 1990s, two-thirds of the adults who were paid only the minimum wage were women.[11] One team of economists has estimated that "the decline in the real value of the minimum wage accounted for roughly a *quarter* to a *third* of the increase in income inequality for . . . women."[12] While an increase in the minimum wage in 1990–91 and again in 1996–97 mitigated this problem, a low minimum wage is one government policy decision that contributes to wage polarization among women workers in the United States.

The fall in the real value of the minimum wage is one reason that the wages of lower-paid women workers declined (when adjusted for inflation) throughout much of the 1990s. This has important consequences for families. Reflecting on the first half of the decade, researchers at the Economic Policy Institute state: "The 1990s . . . saw a notable slowdown in the growth (and, for some groups, even a decline) in hours and earnings of working wives in families with children. Wives' contributions were no longer able to offset the lower earnings of their husbands (whose wages continued to fall except for the top 5% of earners)."[13]

ECONOMIC PARITY OR DISPARITY BETWEEN WHITE AND BLACK WOMEN

In the early days of the current feminist movement, the economic fortunes of black and white women workers were beginning to parallel each other. Married white women were moving into the labor force in greater numbers, bringing their labor force participation rate into line with the traditionally much higher rate of married black women. In addition, black women were moving out of very low paying domestic service positions and finding new jobs in expanding clerical and sales occupations.

The economic status of black women improved when they were able to move out of domestic service jobs. However, it is important to keep the occupational shifts by black women workers in perspective. Black women continued to perform a disproportionate share of other service jobs such as janitors or health care aides. Data show that many black women continue to earn low wages because they are clustered in low-end service jobs.[14] The greater dependence of black women on lower-paying service-sector work is a factor in the wage gap between white and black women.

Still, black women have made important occupational progress in the second half of the twentieth century. Starting in the

1950s, fewer black women followed their predecessors into agricultural and domestic work. The movement of black women out of domestic service jobs into clerical positions in the 1950s through the 1970s led to a convergence in pay between white and black women. By 1975, black and white women had reached near parity; black women earned 98.2 cents for every dollar that white women earned (for full-year, full-time work).[15] In the late 1970s, however, an increasing number of younger white women moved into professional and managerial positions. During the 1980s, a wage gap began to open again. By 1996, black women working full-time year-round earned 85 cents for every dollar earned by white women.[16]

In the 1950s through the mid-1970s, the movement of many black women into the rapidly growing clerical sector was a key factor in the dwindling wage gap between black and white women. However, *within the clerical sector,* there were some rarely examined, underlying patterns that did not bode well for many black women. There is some evidence that black women were disproportionately clustered in the lower-paying, back-office clerical positions. Even more disturbing, a study by economists Marilyn Power and Sam Rosenberg showed that "black women who had achieved good clerical jobs . . . [by the early 1970s] tended not to rise any further. Indeed, by 1980, 41.0 percent of those blacks still in clerical work had fallen in rank." Among the clerical workers whom Power and Rosenberg tracked, almost 20 percent of the white women and none of the black women had moved into higher-paying, *male-dominated* professional positions.[17]

For many black women in the 1980s, clerical jobs were among the best jobs available. This was becoming less true for white women. The difference between white and black women in terms of their dependence on clerical jobs as "good" jobs is important in part because many clerical jobs have been jeopardized by technological developments. Computer and telecommunications technologies are decreasing the need for many types of clerical labor. For example, a United States Department of Labor handbook indicates that there were *fewer* black female typists and file clerks in the early 1990s than there were a decade earlier. The authors rightly point out that office automation played a major role in the elimination of jobs for typists and file clerks.[18] Another study of women working as administrative support personnel in the banking, insurance, and legal services industries in the late 1980s showed that the percentage of clerical workers employed in those key industries was declining. However, the percentage of professionals, officers, and managers in the same industries continued to rise.[19] Industries like banking and legal services have held down the growth of clerical jobs—jobs that have provided good employment opportunities for black women—because technology allows companies to process more information with fewer clerical workers.

A decline in demand for clerical workers is less serious for those women who have opportunities to move into better-paying managerial positions. In their study of the occupational progress of white and black women who were clerical workers in 1972, Power and Rosenberg found that 12.4 percent of the white women had moved into the category "managers, officials, proprietors" by 1980. Only 3.5 percent of black women had made the same transition.[20] Moreover, Anderson and Shapiro found that black women who did obtain professional or managerial jobs had stronger credentials in terms of experience in the workforce and tenure with the present employer than did white women in comparable positions. These two authors remark: "In a sense, [black women] must 'prove themselves'—in order to gain access to a high-paying job."[21]

As late as 1988, a greater proportion of college-educated black women entered the professions rather than managerial positions. Still, the gulf between white women and black women can also be seen when we look at the distribution of these two groups within professional occupations. Black women have been increasing their presence in the professional sector, but they are more likely to be found in traditionally female professions such as nursing, teaching, or social work.[22] Sociologist Natalie Sokoloff found that, during the period from 1960 to 1980, white women were shifting out of the female-dominated professions, but black women were still increasing their share of such jobs. "Black women increased their overrepresentation in female professions while white women [though] still overrepresented cut their share."[23] The female professions in which black women remain clustered offer comparatively less prestige and less pay.

There is another worrisome disparity between black and white women who do hold professional and managerial positions. Those black women who are in management and the professions are more likely to be employed by federal, state, or local government than are their white peers. The public sector was an especially important source of employment for educated black women from 1965 to 1975. During this period, the civil rights movement and associated equal rights legislation led to wider employment opportunities for racial/ethnic women and men just when local and state governments were expanding rapidly. This combination of social trends was important for the employment prospects of college-educated black women. William Carrington and his colleagues report, "At the public sector peak in the early 1970s, over 80% of college-educated black women worked in the public sector, even though this sector accounted for less than 20% of all employment and for only 2% of the employment of white male college graduates."[24] Now, in a political climate that stresses holding down governmental costs and that undercuts affirmative action efforts, we can expect the government sector to provide fewer opportunities for women, particularly black women. In addition, the pressure to reduce welfare costs and to lessen the growth in spending on health care services for the poor will further reduce a group of government jobs that have been important for female professionals and managers. Again, the loss of these government jobs will pose a greater threat to the economic security of black women than of white women. Rita Mae Kelly cites a source that shows that "for white women, the social welfare economy accounted for 39 percent of the job gain between 1960 and 1980; for black women, an even more dramatic 58 percent."[25]

Throughout the 1980s and 1990s, women—as a "generic" category—have made substantial progress in moving into entry-level and middle management positions in the private sector as well as the public sector. However, black women initially made fewer inroads into the managerial ranks. Encouragingly, by the 1990s, black women were finally making some real gains in this area. Between 1988 and 1995, the percentage of black female workers in "executive, administrative and managerial occupations" rose from 7 percent to 9.4 percent. This was a slightly higher percentage increase than that for white female workers. Their percentages went from 11.4 in 1988 to 13.3 in 1995. Interestingly, it was more than double the rate of percentage increase for white male workers, who went from 14.4 percent to 15.4 percent.[26] The recent progress of black women in management is a hopeful development that needs to be encouraged if the economic gap between black and white women is to be lessened.

Still, reaching the level of senior executive remains difficult for women of any race, but it is even more difficult for minority women. A 1992 *Fortune* magazine survey indicated that 95 percent of the most senior female executives are non-Hispanic white women.[27] Continuing economic disparities between white and black women raise important ethical questions for feminist ethicists.

COMPLEX DISPARITIES BETWEEN MALE AND FEMALE WORKERS

Among the economic trends that ought to challenge feminist ethicists are the twisting economic fortunes of male and female workers. One prominent example is the declining gender gap in workers' wages. For many decades, the median wage for women has grown. However, since the 1970s, the median wage for men working full-time, year-round has been shrinking when adjusted for inflation. This means that women have been gaining on men, if the standard for comparison is the median real wage. As economists Francine Blau and Lawrence Kahn have pointed out: "Given the wage inequality in the United States in the 1970s and 1980s, American women may have been swimming upstream in a labor market increasingly unfavorable to low-wage workers."[28]

The wage gap between women and men has been narrowing for longer than is often recognized. A major Rand Corporation study showed that from 1920 to 1980 "the average wages of the entire population of women . . . have increased much faster than the wages of men."[29] This long-term trend of faster wage growth among women than among men is confirmed by a Women's Bureau review of data for the years 1951–92. This review showed that over four decades, women's wages have increased more (on a percentage basis) than men's. However, throughout the century, men have had more education and more work experience, and men commanded higher wages. Therefore, though women's wages were growing more quickly, closing the wage gap between themselves and men was difficult for women.

However, in the 1980s, the wage gap between women and men finally began to close noticeably. In 1980, women working full-time, year-round earned 60.2 cents on the dollar in comparison to men. In 1995, they earned 71.4 cents on the dollar. However, the improvement in this ratio had two causes. Women's wages continued to increase for most of this period; men's wages stagnated or declined. An editorial writer at the *San Francisco Chronicle* notes: "Pay for male workers has dropped 11.7 percent since 1974 while it has risen 6.2 percent for female workers."[30]

The wage losses that men have suffered have contributed more to the lessening wage gap between the sexes than women's wage gains have. Scholars at the Institute for Women's Policy Research calculate that "if men's annual earnings had remained at their 1979 levels in real terms, the female–male earnings ratio would have risen to 63.0 percent rather than 71.4 percent [by 1995]. Thus, nearly three-quarters of the reduction in the wage gap has been due to the falling earnings of men rather than to improvement in women's earnings."[31]

Many female workers have continued to gain ground financially while certain groups of male workers have lost substantial ground. The new information economy in the United States pays a high premium for workers with a better education. The wages for male workers with less than a college education have declined significantly, while the wages for women with a college education have grown. Over the last two decades, the percentage of women receiving a college degree has risen faster than the percentage of men receiving that degree. Thus, the female workforce has become better educated in an economy where the payoff for education at the college level has been increasing.

An important element in the economic advances that some women have made, when compared with some men, is the wage penalty attached to jobs that require a limited education. Much of the economic literature discussing a higher economic return being reaped by better-educated workers discusses only the situation of male workers. However, I contend that better-educated female workers are clearly benefiting as well in an economy where "knowledge" work is more highly valued. Anil Bamezai, in a Rand Corporation study, says:

> The most important change in the structure of wages has been the dramatic rise in the price of skill (that is, schooling and work experience) between 1973 and 1988.

Growth in the demand for highly skilled labor has out-
stripped supply, resulting in an increase in the wage rate of
skilled workers; meanwhile, the demand for relatively unskilled labor has fallen relative to its supply, resulting in a
decrease in the wage rate of relatively unskilled workers.[32]

A growing number of female college graduates have benefited
along with their male peers from a wage bonus for educated labor.

However, since 1979, this increase in pay for better-educated
men has been a complicated subject. A careful look at data from
1979–93 shows that only men who had a postgraduate education
saw a real growth in "average real hourly earnings." The less education a male worker aged twenty-five to sixty-four had, the worse
the erosion in his pay. Still, even men who graduated from a four-
year college were slipping behind slowly. By contrast, women with
a college diploma were able to command higher incomes throughout this period. The percentage increase achieved by women with a
postgraduate education outpaced that of their male peers.[33]

In an important study, economists Chinhui Juhn, Kevin M.
Murphy, and Brooks Pierce have shown that wage inequalities
grew dramatically among male workers between 1963 and 1989.
These economists also attribute the growing wage inequalities to a
growing financial "return" on skills in the United States labor
market in the final quarter of the twentieth century. If 1963—a
good year for United States workers—is used as a baseline, real
wages for the most poorly paid workers fell by 5 percent by 1989.
Over the same period, real wages for the top 10 percent of male
wage earners increased by 40 percent. For less-experienced workers with limited job experience the losses were large. In 1989, "real
wages for the tenth percentile [i.e., the lowest wage earning group]
high school graduates with 1–10 years of experience . . . [were]
about 15 percent lower . . . than wages for the same group in
1963."[34] In the 1970s and 1980s, the poorest-paid young workers
suffered tremendous economic losses: "For the lowest 40 percent
of younger workers, real wages are lower in 1988 than for the cor-
responding group in 1964! Hence for two-fifths of all younger
[male] workers there has been no increase in economic opportunity . . . in about two and one-half decades."[35]

Juhn, Murphy, and Pierce attribute the exploding inequality
among male workers to a variety of factors all loosely covered by

the category of a premium for "skills." Skill may be represented by data on level of education, by years of experience, or by a residual category that these researchers call "unobserved" skills. In other words, these researchers assume that some workers have desirable qualities that motivate employers to pay them more, but that are not captured in traditional data gathered to profile the labor force. They resort to this category of unobserved skills to explain the growing inequalities that exist even in groups of workers who have a similar level of education and experience. For example, there are growing wage inequalities among male workers who have a college education. David Gordon suggests, however, that institutional factors such as the decline in union membership and a decline in the real value of the minimum wage may be more important factors in growing inequalities than an unexplained and unexplainable variation in skills.[36]

Economists Gary Burtless and Lawrence Mishel have shown that during the 1980s there were both lower wages and higher unemployment for male *and female* workers who had less than a high school education. The male high school dropouts were hit even worse than the female ones.[37] This coincides with Juhn, Murphy, and Pierce's analysis of economic data showing that there has been a "fall in demand for low-wage workers. . . . There are simply too *few* low-wage jobs."[38]

WAGES AND JOB TENURE FOR MALE AND FEMALE WORKERS

Men have also been losing ground in job tenure—the number of years they have been employed by their present employer. Often, lower job tenure is related to lower wages. Workers with greater seniority have often benefited from a series of wage increases that have steadily raised their pay. Some economists also theorize that workers gain certain firm-specific knowledge and skills as they continue to work for the same employer over a longer period. These economists speculate that firm-specific skills make a worker more productive, so the employer is willing to pay higher wages to retain workers who have particular skills that are especially valuable to the firm.

As we have seen, the job tenure of men has been falling for almost two decades, while the job tenure of women has been rising. Job tenure has been declining for men in the prime earnings years of thirty-five to fifty-four. Because of waves of early retirement, the job tenure of males fifty-five to sixty-four has declined sharply.

For at least fifteen years, job tenure for women has been rising. Moreover, most of the gain for women has occurred during the 1990s. Much of the job tenure gain has been experienced by women ages thirty-five to fifty-four. Women over forty are now substantially more likely to have worked for an employer ten years or more than were their female predecessors.

Again, job tenure is related to education and, therefore, to perceived job skills. Research by the Department of Labor through the year 1996 shows that both women and men with less than a high school education are experiencing a decline in the average number of years with the same employer. However, men with twelve years or less of schooling have suffered the sharpest losses in job tenure.

There is even some additional, but limited, evidence suggesting that highly educated women are doing well on the job, while even educated men are experiencing more economic strains. This data seems to show that during the recession at the beginning of the 1990s, women were proportionately less likely to lose managerial jobs than were men. It may be that under recessionary pressures, employers substituted lower-cost female labor for higher-cost male labor even in the management ranks.[39] A higher proportion of male managers may have lost jobs because there were many more men among the older managers who were urged to accept early retirement as companies restructured. In addition, sociologist Barbara Baran suggests, based on her observations in the insurance industry: "There is also, however, reason to believe that cheaper female labor is being substituted for more expensive male labor throughout the occupational hierarchy [in the insurance industry] and that women are being used to smooth the process of job redesign and introduction of the new machinery. The professional staffs in the new highly automated personal lines centers of the company where I conducted my intensive case study are so overwhelmingly female that the chief administrator of one joked about being under pressure to develop affirmative action goals for men."[40] Perhaps the pattern of substitution that Baran observed in the insurance industry is beginning to occur in other industries as well.

GENDER, RACE, AND INCOME

Until the 1980s, gender was a more powerful factor than race in determining access to better-paying jobs. White men had the highest annual earnings, but black men earned more than women, white or black. However, the relative wage bonus attached to gender began to shift slowly in the 1980s. United States government data shows that, among the youngest workers (aged sixteen to twenty-four), white female workers surpassed the earnings of black male workers in 1982. Many of those workers would have less than a college education. So, among the youngest workers with more limited skills and experience, white women's prospects have surpassed black men's for more than a decade.

There is some limited evidence that, in the 1990s, a larger segment of white female workers has pulled ahead of black male workers in terms of wages. According to the Women's Bureau, among workers aged twenty-four to fifty-four, white women surpassed the earnings of black men in 1991.[41]

White female workers have surpassed the earnings of black male workers in part because a significant group of minority men has seen its earnings plummet. Gary Burtless and Lawrence Mishel indicate: "Since 1979, the largest growth in low wage work has occurred among minority men. While 25.1% of black men earned poverty level wages in 1979, 38.6% earned poverty wages in 1991. . . . Similarly, among Hispanic men the incidence of poverty level wages grew from 26.6% in 1979 to 43.7% in 1991."[42]

One factor in rising wage inequalities is a change in United States immigration policy. In the recent past, immigration law favored workers who possessed workplace skills that were in high demand. However, changes in immigration law have resulted in an influx of immigrants with less education. An Economic Policy Institute paper says: "One-quarter of the U.S. workers with less than a high school education are now immigrants. Perhaps one-fifth of the recent deterioration in the relative wages of high school dropouts may be due to increased immigration of less skilled workers."[43] Higher immigration rates among persons with less education means more competition for a dwindling number of "low-skill" jobs.

Finally, a hopeful note needs to be added about the quarter-century-long growth in wage and income inequality, particularly among male workers but increasingly among female workers too. Late in 1996, well into the upswing in this current economic recovery, the lowest-paid workers finally began to see their earnings rise. In fact, in the first quarter of 1997, the wages paid to the workers who earned the least rose more (in percentage terms, not in total dollars) than the wages for median earners or for workers who earned the most.

New York Times reporter Louis Uchitelle cautions, however: "The big unknown now is whether the wage gains at the low end will continue long enough to make a meaningful difference for millions of Americans struggling to make ends meet, or whether the raises will be washed away in the next wave of economic distress." [44] There was a modest rise in the wages of the lowest-paid workers late in the economic expansion of the 1980s. In that case, "even that modest gain was wiped out by the 1990–91 recession." [45]

A FEMINIST ANALYSIS OF THE VIRTUE OF SOLIDARITY

Serious economic inequalities exist between black and white women. Increasingly, white female workers are faring better than black male workers. Women with a college or postgraduate education are doing well in a knowledge-based economy, while women, and especially men, with less education are struggling for their economic survival. All these economic trends mean that feminist scholars need to examine the obligations imposed by the virtue of solidarity.

Solidarity among women has been a fundamental, if often implicit, moral norm for the feminist movement. In the history of the feminist movement, there has frequently been a belief that women, as women, share a common oppression. Therefore, a commitment to end one's own oppression as a woman was viewed as a commitment to enhance the well-being of all women. A reliance on a notion of a solidarity shared by women as women based on women's shared suffering as victims of gender oppression was common in the nineteenth- and early-twentieth-century international women's movement. For example, the prominent women's suffrage leader Carrie Chapman Catt appealed explicitly to that "solidarity of a sex" that tied women from many countries together.[46] Some feminists assumed that motherhood was a key, positive experience shared by women. They considered maternal experience the basis for a bond between women that could be an important resource for activities such as an international women's movement for world peace.

However, in recent years, this solidarity among women has been exposed as problematic in, at least, three ways. First, women of color have challenged white women to realize that, because of white racism, women of color experience forms of oppression that do not affect white women in the same way. Indeed, white women often participate in and contribute to the oppression of women of color.[47] Moreover, this critique by women of color is not solely a late-twentieth-century phenomenon. Black women active in the nineteenth- and early-twentieth-century women's movement were critical of the movement's failure adequately to address their concerns insofar as these reflected the experience of racial, as well as gender, oppression.[48]

Second, lesbian feminists pointed out that much of the feminist discourse of the late 1960s and the 1970s assumed that all women were heterosexual women—involved, or potentially involved, as sexual partners with men. Lesbian scholars analyzed a discrete form of oppression—heterosexism. Heterosexism is a type of oppression arising from cultural beliefs and social or economic institutions that enforce heterosexual relationships as the only socially acceptable mode of sexual intimacy. Compulsory heterosexuality harms both straight women and lesbians, but in different ways. Lesbian scholars also claimed a positive range of experiences unavailable in heterosexual women's lives.[49]

Third, as challenges were being raised to the possibility of any "solidarity of sex" encompassing white women and women of color or lesbians and straight women, philosophers and women's studies scholars began to give greater attention to "difference." Partly influenced by post-modernist theory, some feminist scholars have criticized any theoretical work that seems to make universal claims about "women's experience" or about forms of "patriarchal oppression" which threaten every woman in "the same way." These scholars disdain "essentialism"—the intellectual error of conceiving persons and social processes as having an essential structure, i.e., an unchanging core identity that makes them what they are. In particular, some feminist scholars insist that there is no essential "femaleness" that all women share across all other historical, social, cultural, and material differences. Nor is there any essential patriarchal oppression that all women experience in the same way.

For post-modernist feminist critics, if there is any basis for a solidarity in struggle among women, that basis is more particular and shifting than a shared female nature or a shared, universal experience of gender oppression. In such work, always potentially shifting solidarity is brokered based on "particular oppressions in particular locations."[50] Merlyn Mowrey describes this position as one that holds "that patriarchy cannot be resisted in general or as a universal. It can only be resisted in specific discourses, institutions, and structures. The point, however, is that oppression produces resistance, and resistance needs no other legitimation."[51]

One important question, still being debated among feminist scholars, is whether resistance requires moral evaluation or legitimation. Are there any moral norms, such as justice or equality, that are essential moral values for any decent human group or society? Or are there only local struggles against current systems of domination? Or, perhaps, in the end, are there only personal moments of resistance against pressures compelling the "self" to engage repressive behaviors?

I join those who have asserted that the feminist movement must assume a fundamental moral stance in which principles of equal human worth and justice continue to have shared social meaning. In this chapter, I contend that feminists need to reexamine solidarity as one such shared moral norm. Greater attention to the economic polarization that has been discussed in this chapter will require feminists to consider solidarity as a response to the growing economic inequalities among women. Moreover, feminists need to take account of the serious economic vulnerability of many men—and not just men of color. In our current economy, solidarity with those who are economically exploited has to go beyond a solidarity of sex. As some women find themselves in positions of cultural and economic power in the global economy of the late twentieth century, feminist ethicists need to explore a solidarity that includes men as well as women. I suggest that feminist ethicists could profit from examining what has been said about solidarity in Roman Catholic social thought, especially since the publication of *Populorum Progressio* in 1967.

SOLIDARITY IN ROMAN CATHOLIC SOCIAL THOUGHT

A crucial virtue in a world of polarizing economic opportunities is the virtue of solidarity. Solidarity involves a keen awareness of the moral ties that bind human beings to one another and, ultimately, to the other creatures of the earth. Solidarity entails not just a recognition of human interdependence, but also a moral commitment to act to minimize harm and to promote well-being throughout networks of natural and human relationships. Solidarity is a universal moral obligation. In the words of John Paul II, it is "the duty of *all towards all.*"[52]

A central insight in recent Roman Catholic social thought is the recognition, voiced by Paul VI, that "the social question has become worldwide."[53] In Catholic social thought, the "social question" has been—not exclusively, but preeminently—a question of economic justice. When Paul VI acknowledged so explicitly that the social question was now a global one, he also realized that solidarity was an important moral response to this social question. It now becomes imperative for decent people to care about the economic fortunes of the poor and the vulnerable who are at a great distance from ourselves. Our social, historical, technological, and economic interdependence leads to a moral obligation to promote the good of all people throughout the earth.

Moreover, it is not just the economic gulf between the rich nations of the North and the poor nations of the South—the gulf that principally concerned Paul VI in *Populorum Progressio*—that matters. As a global, information society develops, a morally disturbing gulf is emerging between the "knowledge" or financial elites who compete effectively in a global market and the vast number of people with more modest skills and far less wealth who are dependent on the health of their local economies. Rosabeth Moss Kanter is right when she points out the very different life prospects of an international professional and managerial elite and of everybody else. "The global economy," she observes, "threatens to create a class divide between cosmopolitans and locals. Cosmopolitans have portable skills, extensive connections, and wide opportunities. Those who are confined to particular places are more dependent and vulnerable."[54]

In addition, feminist ethicists should no longer concentrate on the gulf between economically privileged white males and everybody else. As I have stressed in this chapter, there is a growing gap between the top female wage earners and many less economically privileged men, including a large group of white men. Solidarity calls us to struggle for a *common* good across all these divides.

Solidarity is an important moral response to the social reality that human beings are increasingly socially and economically interdependent across the globe. The cliché phrase—a global economy—is used so often these days precisely to name a growing sense that economic processes are global in character. An increasing number of ordinary workers are aware that their own economic fortunes are influenced in important ways by economic decisions made around the world.

Not exaggerating the existence of a new, uniquely global, economy in the late twentieth century is important. Trade among groups from different regions of the world has been economically important throughout human history. Capitalism in Europe and the United States has always been international in character. In addition, in recent years, the importance of international trade in the creation and elimination of jobs within any particular nation has often been exaggerated. In an important essay, economists Paul Krugman and Robert Lawrence conclude, for example, that international competition affected the loss of manufacturing jobs, especially unskilled manufacturing jobs, in the United States only modestly over the last several decades.[55] Still, advances in transportation, computer, and communications technologies link global markets together in a new way at the end of the twentieth century. In particular, a world financial market has emerged in which decisions about financial capital are made much more quickly than in previous eras.

Our increasing economic interdependence is experienced in and through our work. Our individual labor connects us to contemporaries with whom we compete or cooperate in our economic endeavors. Many of those contemporaries are not known to us personally. In addition, the work that we do involves knowledge, skills, and tools developed from resources provided by our predecessors. Others have taught us things that form the foundations for our "individual skills." Our individual "employability" has a social past and involves social cooperation in the future.

Paul VI drew a moral lesson from the fact that workers labor in an interdependent economic system. He insisted that we have a moral debt of solidarity arising from the social nature of our work. He declared: "We have inherited from past generations, and we have benefited from the work of our contemporaries: for this reason we have obligations toward all, and we cannot refuse to interest ourselves in those who will come after us. . . . The reality of human solidarity, which is a benefit for us, also imposes a duty."[56]

Our economic interdependence is inescapable. On one level, our global economic interdependence is a sociological fact, but it is not necessarily a moral datum. The virtue of solidarity involves a choice, in the words of John Paul II, to lift our economic interdependence up "to the moral plane."[57]

This virtue of solidarity is not primarily a compassionate feeling toward our fellow human beings. Rather solidarity is a firm attitude of concern for the good of all. John Paul II describes the moral depth of solidarity well:

> [Solidarity] then is not a feeling of vague compassion or shallow distress at the misfortunes of so many people, both near and far. On the contrary, it is *a firm and persevering determination* to commit oneself to the *common good;* that is to say to the good of all and of each individual, because we are *all* really responsible *for all*."[58]

Solidarity is what binds the more powerful and the less powerful in a shared commitment to serve the common good. Moreover, the common good is no longer exclusively local or even national. It is international in scope.

Solidarity is a virtue that helps us to recognize and respect the human dignity of those to whom we are connected economically. John Paul II says: "*Solidarity* helps us to see the 'other'—whether a *person, people, or nation*—not just as some kind of instrument, with a work capacity and physical strength to be exploited at low cost and then discarded when no longer useful, but as our 'neighbor,' a 'helper'" suited to be our valued partner in work.[59] In their letter "Economic Justice for All," the American Catholic bishops say: "Solidarity is another name for this social friendship and civic commitment that make human moral and economic life possible."[60]

The difficulty is that our economic interdependence today is broader, but thinner. We are *not* tied economically to certain others in our local communities. There are no longer enough decent jobs for all those with a limited education. The economic trends discussed in this chapter show that the economy has little need for the labor of younger, poorly educated men. This is one example of the barriers to solidarity that the Catholic bishops acknowledge in a more general way when they state: "Human sin continues to wound the lives of both individuals and larger social bodies and places obstacles in the path toward greater social solidarity."[61]

While solidarity emphasizes an implicitly egalitarian, mutual interdependence, in effect solidarity is closely connected with a moral notion called the "option for the poor." Solidarity is related to a vision of the global common good in which the well-being of each and of all is included. However, a real commitment to this vision of universal well-being means that we must take special note of the plight of the poor and the socially disadvantaged. This is because their economic welfare and their human well-being are most starkly in jeopardy. Unless we respond to global economic changes in just ways, prompted by our moral obligation of solidarity, there will be terrible consequences for the most vulnerable.

In one important passage in *Sollicitudo Rei Socialis,* John Paul II recognizes that economic changes that would promote the good of the most vulnerable and, therefore, the good of all are difficult to make. The struggle for greater economic justice will be long, and it will require strategies adequate in a very complex economic situation. Moreover, in the economic realm, constructive change is even more difficult because of "the *mutability* of very unpredictable and external circumstances." He continues, "Nevertheless, one must have the courage to set out on this path [toward greater economic justice], and, where . . . a part of the journey . . . [has been taken], the courage to go on to the end."[62] A lively sense of our moral interconnections is an important aspect of such perseverance on the path to greater economic justice.

SOLIDARITY, CONFLICT, AND RECONCILIATION

In Roman Catholic ethics, as we have just seen, solidarity is a solidarity of the whole human race. However, in secular discourse, solidarity is frequently described as a virtue that extends only to members of a particular group. One relevant example is the socialist norm of solidarity among workers. According to this norm, workers ought to support one another in the struggle to gain fair treatment from oppressive employers. Solidarity is a virtue that binds workers in loyalty to one another during their conflict with a common enemy—the capitalists.

In contrast, talk about solidarity in Catholic social thought has implicit undertones of reconciliation and social harmony. Solidarity is an attitude that encompasses *all,* seeking the good of *all.* John Paul II contends that, for Christians, solidarity "[takes] on the *specifically Christian* dimension of total gratuity, forgiveness, and reconciliation."[63]

The official documents of Catholic social thought have been quite negative about socialist or Marxist social analysis to the extent that these modes of thought assumed, and even promoted, class antagonisms. There are several reasons for official Catholic antipathy to theories of class conflict. First, the Catholic Church teaches a doctrine of God's saving grace extended to all—rich and poor. The church seeks to encompass within its membership persons from every social class. Any social theory that appears to stress economic divisions seems ultimately inconsistent with the Deity's universal love.

However, it is also true that in both Europe and Latin America, the Roman Catholic Church has had important alliances with members of the most privileged economic class. *Rerum Novarum*— the first document to articulate the modern, magisterial, social thought of the church—was written in a social context of close alliance between the papacy and conservative European elites. Since then, Catholic Church leaders have often been loath to antagonize politically and economically powerful church members whose material and political support make the institutional life of the church far more comfortable.

There is a growing recognition in Catholic social thought of the social barriers that impede solidarity in significant ways. However, there is still a tendency to move quickly to a vision of all working for the good of all, with less emphasis on the struggle among groups that will accompany efforts to promote the well-being of the more vulnerable in twenty-first-century, global capitalism.

A more adequate notion of solidarity will require more careful attention to conflicts arising from factors such as gender, race or ethnicity, or economic interests. Discussing how to decide where preliminary loyalties lie will also be important in situations where universal solidarity is premature. Here the notion that solidarity—lived out in a world of structural economic inequalities—requires an option for the poor is suggestive. In an unjust world, solidarity often involves a practical partiality on behalf of the oppressed as a necessary interim stance to promote ultimately a genuine *common* good.

One aspect of solidarity is its capacity to inspire people to persevere in the struggle for economic justice. However, since solidarity is closely related to courage in a long battle for justice, those practicing solidarity must be prepared for protracted social conflicts in which reconciliation is not within easy reach. If solidarity and harmony are too easily linked, then solidarity may be too diffuse to support any significant economic transformation.

THEOLOGICAL FOUNDATIONS FOR SOLIDARITY

Solidarity is a virtue that concerns the will. Solidarity fuels the will to act for others, particularly vulnerable others. The need for solidarity is particularly sharp in our present social and cultural situation, where we are in urgent need of a transformation in those "spiritual attitudes which define each individual's relationship with self, with neighbor, with even the remotest human communities, and with nature itself."[64]

In an increasingly polarized economic situation, religious foundations provide important support for solidarity. A fundamental moral question in our present economic circumstances is, "Why should I care about the economic problems of other people?" As the economic gulf between a cosmopolitan, professional and managerial elite and workers tied to local businesses grows, it is less and less evident why the cosmopolitans should care about the economic plight of others who live in the community where the cosmopolitans happen to live.

The basic Christian answer to the question "Why care about others?" is that all human beings are bound together by their status as fellow creatures of the one Creator. As Paul VI put it, our common condition as creatures of God produces an obligation to solidarity that is both an outcome of our shared humanity and a religious duty based in our standing as children of God.[65] In other words, solidarity, for a Christian, is provoked by a recognition of the economic "other" as a person who bears the *imago Dei*. Solidarity is based on our moral identification of others as having a dignity and worth as beings who are made in the image and likeness of the Deity.

For Christian believers, Jesus Christ is the central bearer of the divine promise of fulfillment for *all* of humanity and for the *whole* cosmos. Jesus' ministry makes plain that the proclamation of the Deity's future blessedness extended *to all* requires special attention to the message of redemption for those with physical or mental disabilities, those who are poor, and those held captive in a variety of ways. The story of his death and resurrection is a pledge that separation and evil are not the final reality. Christ invites us to share his "solidarity with the whole suffering human race,"[66] confident that the Spirit will catch us up in a future of justice, reconciliation, and wholeness.

Furthermore, Christian faith insists that the Deity is still present among us as Spirit moving in our midst. The Spirit acts to bring about the reign of God/dess, in part through our human struggles for justice and wholeness. Theologian Elizabeth Johnson describes the Spirit as divine power at work in a broken world, providing divine energy for struggles for justice and peace. She views the Spirit as a source of human resistance against evil—a source of "the awesome courage to keep on with the struggle even in the absence of visible success."[67]

As we have seen, solidarity is a virtue rooted in a recognition of the fundamental moral claims arising from human relatedness. Solidarity *as a relational virtue* can be connected, for Christians, with the fundamental relationality of the Christian Deity. In other words, there is a connection between the Christian doctrine of the Trinity and solidarity. As John Paul II says:

> Beyond human and natural bonds, already so close and strong, there is discerned in the light of faith a new model of the unity of the human race, which must ultimately inspire our solidarity. This supreme model of unity . . . is a reflection of the intimate life of God, one God in three Persons.[68]

The Trinity's own life is a model of diversity, equality, and solidarity. Inspired by the characteristics of Trinitarian relationality,

Christians ought to strive to create human relationships characterized by equality and solidarity.

There is a strong connection between solidarity as a virtue in the Christian life and the Christian ritual practice of the eucharist. That connection is made explicit in the documents on Catholic social thought that have been among the key resources for this chapter. In particular, John Paul II contends that solidarity helps us to recognize that all whose work connects them to us are also "made [by God] to be . . . [sharers], on a par with ourselves, in the banquet of life to which all are equally invited by God."[69] The eucharist as a spiritual source for virtues of justice and solidarity will be explored in the last chapter.

5

In the last several decades, the social understanding concerning employment security has changed. While many workers are fortunate enough to have long job tenure with their current employers, there is a diminished social sense that workers are entitled to expect employment security from their employer. The employability contract has emerged as a new social paradigm of the mutual responsibilities between employee and employer. But is the new job contract a fair bargain for the employee? In this chapter, I will set two different strands of moral discourse on business—social contract theory in business ethics and Roman Catholic social thought—in conversation to pursue the question of fairness in the new job contract.

SOCIAL CONTRACT THEORY IN BUSINESS ETHICS

Throughout this book, I have been arguing that there is an implicit social standard for a fair job contract that serves as a moral benchmark to judge aspects of the employment relationship. Further, I have contended that the basic social understanding about economic security as a benefit provided through employment relationships has shifted in a socially significant way. An older job contract that implicitly guaranteed long-term employment security for good workers has been replaced by the employability contract. Increased reliance by major corporations on contingent workers also represents a change in the job contract. Contingent workers are not employees at all, but a type of supplier or a commodity offered by a supplier, such as a temporary help services agency. Since they are not employees, they have no direct claim on any of the benefits offered by the contracting organization. Therefore, contingent workers are excluded entirely from the social job contract, even the new employability contract.

What theories can ethicists use to evaluate the morality of the new job contract and its exclusions? One interesting place to start is with a body of work based in philosophy and applied carefully to business situations, including international business contexts. Philosopher Thomas Donaldson pioneered the concept of applying philosophical social contract theory to business ethics. Donaldson's work, later in collaboration with lawyer and ethicist Thomas Dunfee, provides the best starting point for exploring whether there is ethical substance to the notion of a social contract concerning employment. Can social contract theory applied to business ethics help us get our moral bearings as employment relationships change?

Donaldson and Dunfee argue that there is a moral bargain between society and businesses that gives rise to ethically significant indirect obligations for businesses. Thus they would assert that corporations have moral responsibilities to employees that go beyond the obligations spelled out in written employment contracts, employment law, or collective bargaining agreements. Indeed, for Donaldson, one helpful aspect of "social contract" language is that it points to duties that a corporation has to society or to specific social groups that go beyond legal or (strict) contractual obligations. These indirect duties are, nevertheless, morally significant. In his 1989 book, *The Ethics of International Business*, Donaldson mentions implicit promises of employment security as an example of corporate commitments that "carry moral weight."[1]

In an effort to elucidate the basic social contract between business and society, Donaldson initially performs a thought experiment. He invites his readers to imagine a society in which all productive activity is radically individual productivity. There are no organizations that coordinate joint productive activity. What terms would the surrounding society insist upon before it authorized entities to engage in socially sanctioned joint economic activity? Donaldson asserts that society would insist that the benefits of allowing corporate economic activity must outweigh the negative consequences of permitting such activity.

Then Donaldson makes an interesting choice. He decides that corporations have an impact on the lives of members of society principally through two key economic roles—as employees and as consumers. So Donaldson concentrates on the ways in which society would demand that corporations make employees and consumers better off than those two groups would be if no joint productive activity were permitted.

Given the subject of this book, I am going to concentrate on Donaldson's analysis of the terms of the social contract that apply to persons as workers. Donaldson hypothesizes that potential workers would expect to have enhanced opportunities to contribute to social well-being through joining their efforts with others in cooperative economic ventures. Workers would hope to increase the overall level of social prosperity and to receive appropriate personal financial rewards for their contributions. Assuming that corporate economic activity is more efficient than individual production, workers could expect to derive a greater personal financial return through engaging in joint economic endeavors.

In his original thought experiment described in *Corporations and Morality*, Donaldson gives thoughtful attention to the benefits that persons *as potential employees* would demand in the original contracting position. Donaldson defines an employee as "anyone who contributes labor to the productive process of a productive organization." He then specifically names "laborers" and "part-time support personnel" in a list of examples of employees.[2] A question for Donaldson would be whether temporary workers or contract workers are also "employees" for purposes of Donaldson's social contract analysis. Philip Mattera contends that temporaries and contract workers are not employees, but independent operators in the labor market. In fact, for corporations that is precisely the attraction of some forms of contingent work. "With arrangements like temps, leased employees, and home workers, business is transforming the employment relationship and in a sense dissolving it."[3]

This raises the question, What terms would persons demand for contingent employment in the original contracting position if they knew some persons would be in contingent employment relationships, but they did not know whether they (as individuals) would be in a contingent job once corporate production started? Probably influenced by John Rawls, Donaldson declares that justice requires, among other things, that corporations "avoid any practice that systematically worsens the situation of a given group in society."[4] This raises the question for me whether the forms of contingent employment available to white women and persons of color worsen the economic situations of these groups and, hence, fail to stand up to Rawlsian moral scrutiny.

Donaldson does not specifically discuss contingent employment. He does make some comments about job security for persons in standard employment relationships. In a particularly interesting passage, Donaldson suggests that workers would expect to receive more stable economic support over their life spans through corporate employment. In Donaldson's original position (where all persons are individual producers), a solitary producer who becomes too sick or too old to work faces suffering and possibly death. When individuals band together to form cooperative economic organizations, the organization can buffer these threats for individual workers. Donaldson has in mind corporate benefits such as sick pay or pension plans. In this context, in his 1982 work *Corporations and Morality,* Donaldson offers the example of a fifty-year-old worker who may not be able to work as hard as he did when he was younger, but whose financial responsibilities (for a family) are greater than when he was young. Donaldson then describes the benefits of a long-term corporate employment relationship in which the older worker can expect a higher salary based on seniority even if the worker is less productive with age.[5] Ironically, by the early 1980s, such job security was already under serious economic pressure, particularly for certain manufacturing workers. However, the threat to long-term employment security was not yet clear to the larger society. In 1998, the new job contract in United States society certainly is not consistent with this example provided by Donaldson.

Donaldson argues that his thought experiment leading to the stipulation of basic terms of a social contract between corporations and society is a reasonable undertaking because it clarifies the minimum that business owes to society. Donaldson supports his claim that corporations have duties to society that go beyond just obeying society's laws by pointing to the benefits that any corporation receives from society—benefits that are essential for the existence of the corporation. He reminds his readers that any corporation exists "only through the cooperation and commitment of society. It draws its employees from society, sells its goods to society, and is given its [legal] status by society."[6] In this passage, Donaldson comes close to the Roman Catholic teaching about the "social mortgage" on productive capital that I will discuss below.

Thomas Dunfee has provided an important refinement of the social contract theory of business ethics through a discussion of "extant social contracts."[7] Extant social contracts are the moral understandings actually shared by "communities or groups of individuals with common goals or values."[8] According to Dunfee, the provisions of an extant social contract "are empirically discoverable, and should often be well known within the community."[9] However, extant social contracts are often implicit social understandings—nowhere specifically defined in precise, written terms. He declares that businesses have a serious moral obligation to honor such extant social contacts, unless the terms of a specific social contract violate basic moral norms as determined by standard philosophical systems of analysis.[10] He and Donaldson also cite empirical evidence that business managers do recognize a moral obligation to comply with the basic moral standards of the communities in which they live, i.e., to honor existing social contracts.[11] Extant social contracts do not completely define the moral obligations of businesses, but "they form a part of the overall ethical framework" that executives and members of the corporate boards ought to take into account when assessing the corporation's social responsibilities.[12]

Extant social contracts, according to Dunfee, are real shared social understandings. Therefore, one ought to be able to point to concrete evidence that such widely shared social expectations actually exist. Dunfee examines norms that vary from culture to culture regarding such practices as gift giving in a business context or buying stock based on information that is not publicly available (insider trading). For the purposes of this book, is there an extant social contract concerning employment security that is now being renegotiated? Any extant social contract concerning employment security would have specific features in the United States. There is evidence that workers in many countries value employment security. In some of the European countries, there are elaborate, explicit social mechanisms that protect employment security for workers. However, in the United States, the government provides little support for a worker's claim to continuing employment based on adequate job performance. While job security might be negotiated in collective bargaining agreements, long-term employment in return for acceptable job performance has remained an implicit feature of many desirable employment arrangements in the United States.

In discussing the present lessening of employment security, many writers spontaneously use the language applied to a breach of a social contract. A writer for a human resources journal describes the contemporary situation in this manner: "An entire generation of workers woke up one morning to learn the contract they thought they had signed up for—steady employment with regular promotions—had been torn up overnight. Now, there's not only no career growth to look forward to, there's no immediate job security either."[13] Scholar John Paul MacDuffie claims: "Employment security for white-collar employees in large U.S. corporations has almost always been implicit, *and this is testimony to how fundamental the expectation of long-term employment, from both company and employee, has been.*"[14] Economist Paul Osterman says: "For nearly every group of employees the terms and conditions of employment have changed, in many cases quite dramatically." He continues that for most workers, including managerial workers, there is greater "insecurity even in the face of declining unemployment rates."[15] Labor leaders John Sweeney and Karen Nussbaum declare: "Even business insiders now worry that the old social contract [job security and a share of the benefits of increased productivity in return for hard work] has not been replaced by any new policies that give people incentives to work productively."[16] Addressing questions of economic justice, even the Roman Catholic bishops of the United States express the hope that they can contribute toward "a renewed social contract between employers and employees."[17]

A study by sociologist Sheryl Tynes contains other pertinent material. She conducted in-depth interviews with white-collar workers, particularly managers, at four pairs of corporations that had eliminated white-collar jobs as a result of mergers and acquisitions. She asserts: "Nearly all respondents had operated for most of their lives in a work environment that explicitly or implicitly promised job security; suddenly they were faced with a different set of expectations." She terms this "a major breach of contract."[18]

One executive who had gone through a hostile takeover was interviewed by Tynes. He indicated that he was troubled by his inability to protect the interests of relatively long-term employees of the original company. He said: "It really is a tough situation to see people who have given 5 to 20 years of their life to a company, and suddenly there's no more company, no more job."[19] I infer from this statement that this senior executive implicitly viewed long-time employees as having some moral claim to employment security and that he was troubled by the original company's inability to protect the interests of these employees in continued employment.

Moreover, in Tynes's study, many of the personnel *who were retained* during mergers or acquisitions lost their trust in any implicit job contract offering long-term employment in return for good job performance. In fact, one highly placed executive who kept his job during the merger told Tynes that he would "probably never again trust an employer to reward me with a job if I continue to perform." Another executive who left and started his own business reported that "job security is totally a thing of the past." He offered his own version of the employability contract when he said that economic security was something that a person has to create for himself. The only type of economic security that he could envision was security based completely on personal "credentialing, and knowledge, and self-worth."[20]

While nearly all of Tynes's respondents had changed their expectations about their ability to rely on their employer to provide *long-term* employment security, they had differing perceptions about how the mergers or acquisitions were likely to affect their immediate job prospects. Almost half of Tynes's respondents said that their level of job security remained the same, over 27 percent viewed their positions as less secure, and 18 percent said they had improved job security. (If a company in financial difficulty merged with [or was acquired by] a stronger company, some workers from the first company *would* gain greater job security.)[21]

I have concentrated here on evidence in the United States social context that there was a microsocial contract that promised long-term employment in return for good job performance. If such a contract exists or existed, the national level is probably the largest scale where it could have meaning.

There is additional sociological and economic evidence that shows that United States workers value employment security highly. For example, one study of human resources executives found that employment security was the third most urgent personnel question facing companies in the early 1990s (ranking just behind benefits and wages).[22] A stream of stories about specific labor negotiations in the *Monthly Labor Review* indicates that providing employment security for their members has been a top priority of labor unions during many collective bargaining sessions.[23]

In addition, there is evidence that workers or potential workers in other nations also value employment security highly.[24] Such evidence supports the contention that employment security is a good that potential employees would demand of corporations in some original contracting position.

In this discussion, I have concentrated on the benefits that the worker got from the old employment contract and the losses for the worker in the new contract imposed by management. However, corporations also stand to lose employee commitment to working hard to advance the corporation's aims. As a result of imposing the employability contract broadly, organizations face the problem of gaining employee "commitment to the success of the organization when the organization itself has reduced its commitment to the individual."[25]

CONSENT AND THE MORALITY OF THE NEW JOB CONTRACT

Several social scientists who have discussed the changing implicit employment contract between employers and white-collar workers describe a situation in which the terms of the contract appear to have been unilaterally changed by employers for the employers' benefit. Shari Caudron describes workers as having awakened one morning to find that the employment contract had been changed. Tynes talks about loyal white-collar workers who "were suddenly faced with *shredded promises* and shifting rules."[26] Finally, economist Lester Thurow says: "The second wave of downsizing [in 1993 among profitable firms] can also be seen as the sudden imposition of a new tougher social contract between owners and workers."[27] From the perspective of social contract theory in business ethics, the notion that extant social contracts could be changed unilaterally by the more powerful party in a manner that primarily promoted the interests of the more powerful party is disturbing.

Indeed, Thomas Dunfee claims that extant social contracts "derive their obligatory nature from consent."[28] He does acknowledge that persons sometimes find themselves confronted by an existing social contract without having an initial chance to influence the terms of that contract. In a 1994 joint work, Donaldson and Dunfee claim that consent can be presumed when persons continue to work for a company, as long as they could have left the company if it was necessary to dissociate themselves from some practice that they found morally unacceptable. The authors say that economic situations in which persons are coercively prevented from leaving are rare.[29]

In 1991, Dunfee did acknowledge that people do not always have realistic opportunities to withdraw from communities whose social contracts contain provisions that they personally find objectionable. Dunfee recognized the role of "economic necessity and the presence of viable alternatives in determining whether consent can be implied from a failure to leave the community."[30] In the 1994 essay, Dunfee and Donaldson also say that situations in which some parties to an existing social contract have severely limited economic alternatives are "hard-to-classify cases." They note that poor workers, particularly those living in areas of high unemployment, face circumstances that pose a difficult problem for their social contract theory, but in this essay they pull back from "attempting to resolve this difficult issue."[31]

Consent can be a crucial, but difficult, point in such social contract theories. As Michael Keeley points out: "Unambiguous signs of consent are not that common in organizations and other communities."[32] An important element here is that an employment relationship endures over time. It is not a one-time bargain, such as the purchase of some quickly consumed product like a bar of soap. There is more opportunity for the terms of the job "bargain" to change over time. This is exactly what many long-time employees of some corporations feel has happened to them. The terms of the implied employment contract were changed unilaterally by the employer, with employment security eliminated as a provision.

In assessing the new job contract, one factor to be considered is whether under terms of global capitalism a growing group of workers face choices that are seriously constrained. In an increasingly interdependent global labor market, some workers' employment opportunities are influenced not just by the unemployment rate in their region or country, but also by the existence of a global labor pool in which there are many unemployed workers in other countries. Lester Thurow asserts, for example, "Raw labor (the willingness to sacrifice leisure) . . . can, in any case, be bought very cheaply when there is an entire globe of poor underemployed workers to draw upon."[33] In addition, certain groups of skilled workers such as computer programmers increasingly offer their labor as a commodity in an international labor market. They face serious competition from programmers in nations such as India. This suggests that we will need increasingly to look at global labor market constraints on many United States workers when we try to assess their "consent" to various aspects of the extant social contract governing employment relationships.

Donaldson alluded briefly to this problem in *The Ethics of International Business*. While defending the right of workers freely to associate with one another as members of labor unions, Donaldson discussed some difficulties facing unions today. He said, "The twin phenomena of commercial concentration and the globalization of business, both associated with the rise of the multinational, have tended to weaken the bargaining power of labor."[34]

Earlier, Donaldson had briefly considered how corporations, which have indirect moral obligations to employees, could accurately assess the needs of their employees. In this context Donaldson said: "Frequently unions serve to represent employee interests to management."[35] However, he acknowledged the moral failings of unions, offering as an example union complicity with racial segregation of jobs—maintaining the best jobs for white union members. Importantly, Donaldson recognized the low level of union representation in the early 1980s, a situation that has only worsened since Donaldson wrote *Corporations and Morality*. This loss of union bargaining power has more implications for the social contract concerning employment than Donaldson and Dunfee have yet explored.

Edward J. Conry highlights a more pessimistic view of the freedom of workers to withhold consent from unpalatable social contracts with businesses. He says, "And in business, the exchange of a salary for obedience is often a duressive relation. So duress may systematically undermine the moral legitimacy of 'consented to' norms as moral guides in business organizations."[36] This bears some similarity to Michael Keeley's discussion of the legal concept of contracts of adhesion.[37] The law recognizes that special scrutiny is required in some instances where less powerful parties "consent" to standardized contracts drawn up by much more powerful parties. An example of a contract of adhesion is certain standardized warranties or rental or lease agreements. Keeley refers to contracts of adhesion to highlight the moral difficulties that can arise when parties to a contract have very unequal access to social resources, such as the advice of sophisticated lawyers.

Sheryl Tynes offers some interesting empirical data concerning the complexity of "voluntary" choice or consent as concepts relevant for sorting out the morality of the new job contract. Tynes reports that more than 20 percent of her subjects "left voluntarily" when their companies went through mergers or acquisitions. She immediately cautions, however, that the categories she used to characterize her subjects' choices—"stay, leave voluntarily, leave involuntarily . . . implied 'choice,' which the interviews revealed as problematic."[38] She reports that many of those who left "voluntarily" did so because they thought that they faced a substantial risk of losing their jobs anyway or because they expected a loss of autonomy or a reduction in pay or benefits.

I suggest that, when assessing the morality of the new "employability" contract, it is important to look carefully at the unequal power held by large employers and differing groups of workers. Certain knowledge workers who can command and manipulate crucial information may be able to bargain for a viable employability contract. It is in the best interests of the employer and such knowledge workers for the business to provide these employees with opportunities to maintain their skill. Workers with less specialized knowledge and skills may have much less opportunity to participate effectively in a social renegotiation of the terms of the employment contract.

An open question is whether many workers have in any morally meaningful sense consented to the new employability contract. One pertinent empirical question would be whether there are still many companies that are offering workers work on the old terms—a secure job in return for hard work and satisfactory performance. Do most workers have a genuine opportunity to leave companies moving to the employability contract and to find employment with employers offering greater employment security?

Michael Keeley has expressed serious concern about rooting the moral authority of "social contracts" in the notion of informed consent granted by all parties to the social contract. He points out enduring difficulties with the notion of consent, particularly but not exclusively the practice of inferring "tacit" consent from continued participation in a social or business relationship. Keeley points out that social contract thinkers frequently have other fundamental value commitments that are below the surface of their social contract analysis. For example, Keeley himself emphasizes the importance of respect for persons as a fundamental moral norm. The principle of equal respect stands behind versions of the social contract where "an attempt is made to ensure the satisfaction of such [basic] interests for each and every participant." Keeley takes an even more interesting position when he continues: "This means giving first priority to participants whose fundamental interests might be in jeopardy."[39]

ROMAN CATHOLIC SOCIAL THOUGHT AND THE NEW JOB CONTRACT

Roman Catholic social thought puts its emphasis on the sort of basic ethical principle that Keeley suggests serves as the basis for social contract analysis applied to organizational ethics. The Roman Catholic social tradition begins explicitly with the principle of the dignity of human beings as persons made in the image and likeness of the Deity. A key implication of this starting point for economic ethics is articulated by Pope John Paul II. John Paul II insists labor is not just another factor similar to financial capital or raw materials as an input in production. He insists upon "the principle of the priority of labor over capital."[40] The corollary of this principle is the refusal to see a human being in the workplace as a commodity to be used in carefully measured amounts in order to achieve the greatest productivity at the least cost.

Donaldson and Dunfee would certainly agree with the principle of the respect owed to human persons in any business situation. These two authors have developed a theory about the existence of certain fundamental moral principles, which can be used to evaluate extant social contracts and other business practices. Interested in articulating a theory that can be used in international business operations, they call these fundamental principles hypernorms—i.e., norms that supersede the cultural norms of any given society. Prominent among Donaldson and Dunfee's hypernorms is "the obligation to respect the dignity of each human person."[41]

A fundamental moral stance protective of the human dignity of the worker requires a critical moral assessment of the treatment accorded workers under any job contract. Such positions refuse to accept neoliberal forms of contract theory that argue that any contract is fair if its terms are voluntarily accepted by rational parties.

From the neoliberal perspective, a worker's labor is a commodity to be sold for wages and other benefits on the labor market. The price of a worker's labor will be determined by what the labor market will bear for workers with particular skills. Often this view entails the notion that there is a unified labor market in which all workers offer their services to all employers. Workers have various personal preferences concerning the terms of employment. Workers may accept a job with lower wages than they could receive from another employer in order to satisfy the workers' preference for features such as job location or hours. It is common to argue that female workers accept various offers of contingent employment because they have personal preferences that lead them to subordinate their workplace interests to private, domestic responsibilities.

When Pope Leo XIII wrote the first social encyclical *Rerum Novarum,* in 1891, he had to rebut precisely such a liberal theory of fair employment contracts. According to the liberals of Leo's day, a contract to employ an unskilled laborer at a poverty-level wage was a fair contract because the laborer had freely chosen to accept work at that wage level.

Leo put the liberal fiction of a free contract between employer and employee in perspective when he realistically assessed the constraints faced by persons who must provide for their families' economic survival through their labor power. Leo recognized that it was "a mere abstract supposition" that a worker was free to accept or reject an employment contract on any of a wide variety of terms, including a low rate of pay. Rather, wage labor was "necessary" for the survival of members of the working class. A job and decent wages were the only way in which such persons could obtain "what is required in order to live."[42]

Viewing the results of purportedly "free" bargaining between powerful factory owners and poor workers during the early stages of industrial capitalism, Leo recognized that economic vulnerability undermined any notion of genuinely voluntary bargaining between employer and potential employee. In the real world of the 1890s, when a poor worker accepted a harsh employment contract because he or she saw no better alternatives, the worker was "the victim of force and injustice."[43] In the 1960s, Pope John XXIII reiterated that labor contracts that violate justice and equity remain immoral, "even though they are entered into freely on both sides."[44]

Despite his strong defense of the property rights of capitalists and his assumption that social hierarchies reflected the will of God, Leo insisted that the principle of justice determined basic duties that employers owed to workers despite what workers might be willing to accept. Leo focused especially on the workers' right to a living wage. For this pope, a living wage was the cornerstone of economic security for a worker and the worker's family.

Leo had the unrealistic idea that a living wage should allow a male breadwinner whose family lived frugally to save enough money to buy a small homestead. Relying on an agrarian ideal that was inconsistent with the new industrial order, Leo envisioned a world where families were secure because they could always turn to subsistence farming if necessary. The specifics of Leo's theory of a living wage were inadequate for his time and are even more inadequate in the postindustrial age.

However, a crucial moral insight remains from Leo's discussion of a living wage—one that has been affirmed by all later Roman Catholic thought. Workers, as human beings, are entitled to justice in employment relationships. Justice requires that employment relationships be structured in a way that enables all workers to gain modest economic security for themselves and their dependents. Interpreting a living wage as a claim to a reasonable measure of economic security, Leo's warning to the employers of his day remains a moral challenge to the employers of our time:

Rich men and masters should remember this—that to exercise pressure for the sake of gain, upon . . . [the economically vulnerable], and to make one's profit out of the need of another, is condemned by all laws, human and divine. To defraud any one of wages that are his due is a crime that cries out to the avenging anger of heaven.[45]

I interpret the Roman Catholic principle of a living wage to include a demand for modest economic security. For the vast majority of people living in industrial and postindustrial societies, wages and pensions are still the basic source of economic security. Therefore, there is a key connection between employment security and economic security. In order to provide a decent living for themselves and their dependents, most workers need to remain employed throughout most of their prime adult years. Employers have a responsibility to devise forms of the job contract that are consistent with employment security over the span of a work life. It remains a pressing social question whether the new employability contract is consistent with employment security over the span of a work career for ordinary workers. When evaluating the new employment contract, we need to pay much closer attention to the situation of Donaldson's hypothetical fifty-year-old worker, who might be slowing down (or who might not have cutting-edge knowledge and skills) but whose family's economic needs are pressing.

The United States Catholic bishops recognize that in some businesses and industries, global capitalism is putting severe pressure on *employers* who want to offer fair terms of employment, including reasonable employment security. With investment capital and sophisticated technology readily available to employers in nations with widely diverse employment costs, these labor costs become "the main variable in the cost of production." This set of economic conditions "put[s] enormous pressure on U.S. firms to cut wages, relocate abroad, or close."[46] The freedom of conscientious employers to enter into a fair employment bargain is sometimes compromised by world economic conditions.

MORAL RESTRAINTS REQUIRED OF FINANCIAL CAPITAL

Competition for return on investment capital in a global financial market is placing constraints on all parties to the new job contract. In this context, one strength of the Roman Catholic social tradition is its willingness forthrightly to place moral restraints on the rights of capital. The Roman Catholic tradition denies that investors and managers have a right to pursue productive investments based exclusively on obtaining the most profitable rates of return. In an address to the Latin American bishops in Puebla, Mexico, John Paul II found a striking metaphor to describe the moral accountability that Catholic social thought demands from capital on behalf of society. He spoke of a "social mortgage" on capital and all other forms of private property.[47]

John Paul II takes the strong position that the only basis for a morally legitimate claim to control of productive property is that owners and managers organize the use of machinery and investment capital in a fashion that creates jobs for labor and useful goods for the community.[48] It is interesting to note that this agrees with the result of Thomas Donaldson's thought experiment generating the basic social contract. Donaldson argued that society allows productive organizations to exist because they benefit members of society as workers and consumers. John Paul II stated the responsibilities of financial investors to workers forcefully when he told an audience of businesspeople in Mexico, "The only legitimate title for owning the means of production is that they serve labor. Hence one of your greatest responsibilities must be that of creating jobs."[49] The pope immediately continued by speaking about a just wage, so by implication capital has a responsibility to create jobs on fair terms.

The powerful image of a social mortgage is relatively recent in Catholic thought, but the basic insight that it captures has deep roots. Even in the midst of his vigorous defense of capitalists' absolute right to their private property, Leo XIII reminded his audience that the economic prosperity of society was based in great measure on the "most efficacious and altogether indispensable" efforts of workers. He concluded that the significant contributions of workers to national wealth made it incumbent on society to protect the legitimate claims of workers to safe working conditions and fair pay.[50]

The insight that profits and productive property are not created solely by wise investment decisions but rather in a synergy with the labor power of workers is a thread through all subsequent Catholic social thought. In 1986, the U.S. Catholic bishops said that the wealth produced by business creates a social inheritance that is similar to a social trust fund. This social trust fund, generated by social contributions to business wealth, should be administered to promote the common good. The bishops argued that "owners and managers have not created this capital on their own. They have benefited from the work of many others and from the local communities that support their endeavors. They are accountable to these workers and communities when making decisions."[51]

As a counterpoint, in *Centesimus Annus,* John Paul II gives specific attention to the contribution of the skillful executive or entrepreneur who creates astute strategies to meet consumer demands. He says, "It is precisely the ability to foresee both the needs of others and the combination of productive factors most adapted to satisfying those needs that constitutes another important source of wealth in modern society."[52] Economic initiative and entrepreneurial talent have the potential to make a genuine contribution to the common good and hence deserve an appropriate share of the economic benefits created. Still, the social mortgage on corporate wealth gives workers and their communities a basis for holding managers and investors morally accountable for the social consequences of their decisions.

KNOWLEDGE AS A KEY FORM OF PROPERTY

Starting in the 1960s, Catholic social thought began to incorporate the realization that in advanced industrial societies specialized skill or knowledge can be an important economic resource of great value to workers. In *Mater et Magistra,* John XXIII offered the observation that professional skills may be a more important source of continuing economic security for middle-class workers than material forms of private property, such as land.[53] John Paul II, particularly in *Centesimus Annus,* explicitly acknowledged the growing role of specialized knowledge as a source of economic security and wealth in postindustrial society. He too compared these skills to land as a source of economic security.[54] Both John XXIII and John Paul II probably compared knowledge with land ownership because in *Rerum Novarum* Leo XIII's ringing defense of a right to private property was closely connected to Leo's (nostalgic and unrealistic) vision of small landholdings as the basis for economic security for families.

In a more realistic way, John Paul II draws the conclusion that it is increasingly important for society to provide all its members with the education and training that enable individuals to compete for jobs in an information economy. John Paul II recognizes that labor markets can serve as an efficient mechanism for allocating *human* resources. But this is true only insofar as persons have an opportunity to develop "marketable" knowledge and skills. The pope is all too aware that there are millions of poor people around the world, including people in the advanced industrial nations, who lack the education to get good jobs in a global information age. With "no way of entering the network of knowledge and intercommunication," these disadvantaged persons see that the economic advances of contemporary global capitalism are taking place "over their heads," leaving them on the impoverished margins.[55]

We need to build upon this more recent acknowledgment in Catholic social thought of the crucial economic value of knowledge. Skill and knowledge are types of personal economic resources that can be degraded quickly in the current situation of rapid cultural and technological change. This raises some important social questions. Do employers have an obligation to help employees whose knowledge or skills are becoming obsolete? This appears to be the core of the employer's obligation under an employability contract, but as we have seen it is unclear that employers are consistently providing skill and knowledge "upgrades" for all employees. Under the employability contract, what level of responsibility do employees assume to increase their own knowledge and skills? Is the level of individual accountability for developing new skills a fair responsibility or an unjust burden? What responsibility does society have to assist workers whose knowledge base or employment skills have become obsolete?

Workers who lack the knowledge or skills to get and to hold a decent job are one example of the socially vulnerable groups whose plight receives moral priority in Roman Catholic thought. Roman Catholic social thought does not adopt an impartial standpoint; it adopts a moral stance of advocacy for the socially disadvantaged and the economically vulnerable. The contemporary phrase that describes this stance is "the option for the poor."

The Option for the Poor

Catholic social thinkers assert that justice requires a special concern for the poor and the socially marginal because they are more vulnerable to injustice and various types of dehumanization. Even in *Rerum Novarum*, the socially conservative Leo XIII concluded that the state had a special obligation to protect working people from injustice at the hands of wealthy employers.

First, Leo asserted that one basic purpose of any legitimate government is to provide equal protection for the basic rights of its citizens. In one sense, the rich and the poor are entitled to equal regard from the government. But Leo was realistic enough to recognize that the rich usually have numerous means at their disposal to protect their rights if those rights are threatened. The poor, however, have few personal means to seek vindication for their rights. Therefore, the state ought to guard the rights of the poor with special diligence. According to Leo: "When it comes to protecting the rights of individuals, the poor and helpless have a claim to special consideration."[56]

Still, Leo was so much an elitist that he followed this declaration of a special concern for the poor with the advice that all would benefit if the government made the protection of private property its first priority. Recall, however, that Leo hoped that the working class would be able broadly to own property in the form of small family farms. Leo denounced proposals to socialize any form of private property or to redistribute wealth held as private fortunes. Leo believed that proposals to socialize or redistribute property were motivated by "covetous greed." Moreover, he declared that socialists sought to promote such schemes "under the pretext of futile and ridiculous equality."[57]

Despite its nostalgic and conservative elements, the enduring moral power of *Rerum Novarum* is to be found in Leo XIII's vigorous advocacy on behalf of poor workers exploited in the early stages of industrial development throughout Europe and in the Americas. The desperate condition of many among the working class and the huge disparity between the wealth of a few industrialists and the poverty of the mass of workers were the moral issue that called forth this first social encyclical. Leo's first concern was for the masses in the working class who were enduring "a yoke little better than slavery itself."[58]

The importance of adopting a standpoint of advocacy for the poor was much more explicitly articulated in Roman Catholic ethics around 1970, under the influence of Latin American liberation theology. In 1968, the Latin American bishops convened for a Second General Conference in Medellín, Colombia. Surveying a continent where the vast majority of the people lived in poverty and where there was a huge economic gap between the dire poverty of the masses and the enormous wealth of a very few, the bishops committed themselves to give preference in their ministry to the needs of the poor. As Donal Dorr describes it, at Medellín the Latin American bishops "accepted the obligation to be in solidarity with the poor and marginalised."[59] In so doing they created a moral challenge for the international church, particularly the church in the wealthier nations of Europe and North America.

In *Octogesima Adveniens* (Call to Action, 1971), Pope Paul VI took up this theme, declaring, "The Gospel instructs us in the preferential respect due to the poor and the special situation they have in society: the more fortunate should renounce some of their rights so as to place their goods more generously at the service of others."[60] In *Laborem Exercens,* John Paul II commits the church to solidarity with movements for justice for workers as a manifestation of the church's mission to be the "church of the poor." He says specifically that faithfulness to the witness of Jesus is the source of this duty to be in solidarity with workers and the poor.[61]

The implications of this stance are set forth even more fully in the United States Catholic bishops' letter "Economic Justice for All." In this pastoral letter the bishops emphasize frequently that the measure of justice achieved by a society is assessed most adequately by evaluating the situation of the poor. They proclaim: "We can best measure our life together by how the poor and the vulnerable are treated." They connect this priority for the poor to its biblical roots, continuing, "This is not a new concern for us. It is as old as the Hebrew prophets, as compelling as the Sermon on the Mount."[62]

In recent Catholic thought, the category of the poor is sometimes broadened to include those who are socially marginalized and disadvantaged in a variety of ways not limited to economic poverty. A typical example of this expansion of the category of "the poor" is found in *Laborem Exercens,* where John Paul II says,

"And the 'poor' appear under various forms . . . in many cases they appear as a result of the violation of the dignity of human work."[63] In view of this broader understanding of "the poor," I would ask whether older men who have been involuntarily pushed out of the labor force are examples of the "poor," even if they are members of the middle class who have lost managerial and professional positions.

The option for the poor has remained a controversial moral stance, particularly for the church in the more advanced industrial economies, where a majority of the Catholic faithful are members of the middle class. John Paul II, demonstrating the tendency in Catholic thought to stress inclusion and social harmony, has assured his hearers that the "preferential option for the poor . . . is never exclusive or discriminatory toward other groups."[64] Indeed, if the option for the poor suggested that the Deity was a partisan for the poor, then the question could be raised whether divine love and salvation were also extended to more economically privileged persons. Faced with this implied question, John Paul II has made a special effort to say that the implication of the option for the poor is *not* that the Deity loves the poor more or that salvation is offered in some preferential way to the poor.

This pope has fiercely resisted any interpretation of church teaching that appears to set class against class. Such efforts seem to him to mirror a Marxist doctrine of class struggle that he firmly repudiates. Speaking before the Latin American bishops in Puebla in 1979 (on the tenth anniversary of Medellín), he insisted that the good news of Jesus Christ was that Christ "opens his message of conversion to all, and he does not exclude even the publicans." John Paul here depicts the ministry of Jesus as one offering a "complete and integral salvation through a love that brings transformation, peace, pardon, and reconciliation." Those who labor for justice in solidarity with the poor must remember, the pope counsels, that repentance and conversion are possible for all. The advocates on behalf of the poor must also promote forgiveness and reconciliation with the privileged and the oppressor.[65]

It is clear in the address at Puebla that John Paul II is making an integral connection among God's inclusive love, an attitude of solidarity with the poor that is consistent with social harmony, and a Christian "vocation to concord and unity that must banish the

danger of warfare" from the Latin American continent.[66] Recent
events such as the armed insurgence and repressive, paramilitary
violence in the Chiapas region of Mexico in 1998 make John
Paul's concern about the relationship among solidarity, justice, and
peace a realistic and relevant one.

There is a potential conflict between the preferential option for
the poor and the value of social inclusivity. The United States
Catholic bishops attempt to avoid social divisiveness while promoting special concern for the poor by asserting that "a fundamental 'option for the poor'" remains a necessary element in
achieving a morally defensible communal life before the Divine
Being.[67] The bishops interpret a moral standpoint based on an option for the poor as a strategic choice in the service of a genuine
common good and a morally vibrant community life. The bishops
appeal to a shared national, cultural value of "justice for all," emphasizing that justice *for all* requires special attention to the claims
of the poor and the vulnerable, who are at special risk to be deprived of justice. This is the context in which to understand the
bishops' assertion that *"the obligation to provide justice for all
means that the poor have the single most urgent economic claim
on the conscience of the nation."*[68]

A central concern for the needs of the poor is closely related to
a judgment in *Mater et Magistra* that large disparities of wealth are
morally disturbing, particularly if the gap in wealth is expanding,
not closing. According to John XXIII, economic growth is a social
good that needs to be coupled with widespread distribution of the
benefits of prosperity. He insists that social justice requires that *"all
classes of citizens [should] . . . benefit equitably from an increase in
national wealth.* Toward this end, vigilance should be exercised and
effective steps taken that class differences arising from disparity of
wealth not be increased but lessened so far as possible."[69]

A moral posture that is suspicious of large and growing inequalities of income and wealth led the United States Catholic
bishops to be uneasy even in the midst of national prosperity in
1996. On the tenth anniversary of their pastoral letter on the economy, they surveyed a United States economy showing "remarkable
strength and creativity, but with . . . economic growth distributed
too inequitably." They were disturbed by their perception of a society divided into three very unequal groups. The first are those

who are "prospering and producing in a new information age, coping well with new economic challenges." The second group are those members of the middle class who are "squeezed by declining real incomes and global economic competition," and who are fearful about a loss of jobs and job benefits such as health insurance. The third are "an American underclass" struggling to obtain the bare necessities of life—"their children growing up desperately poor in the richest nation on earth."[70] Those same children are also likely to be deprived of educational opportunities that would give them some chance to move into one of the other two groups. Such wide and widening inequalities seriously undermine solidarity and a commitment to the common good, which are key values in the bishops' eyes.

While federal legislation to raise the minimum wage and a tight labor market created by years of economic growth have reduced these social inequalities slightly since 1996, the bishops' basic description of an economically divided society is still apt. The United States Catholic bishops say that justice does not require "absolute equality in the distribution of income and wealth." They acknowledge the importance of economic incentives to spur hard work and creativity and they recognize that greater rewards motivate persons to take risks that end up benefiting the larger society. However, they see it as morally disturbing that some persons possess great wealth while many other persons lack the necessities of life. They are especially concerned that "extreme inequalities are detrimental to the development of social solidarity and community."[71]

Labor Flexibility, Fairness, and Femininity

Some of the growing economic inequalities in contemporary society are tied to an increased use of contingent labor arrangements around the globe. I would suggest that social contract theory and Roman Catholic social thought may not be fully adequate tools for the task of morally analyzing these developments. In addition, I suggest that their shortcomings in this area are rooted in their failures to take gender into account in insightful ways.

Greater use of contingent workers has made the United States economy more "flexible." Many commentators claim that greater flexibility is a key reason why the United States economy has been able to generate so many net new jobs and why unemployment rates are their lowest in a quarter century. Social contract theory might suggest that more flexible employment relations are fine as long as employees and employers give voluntary informed consent to a contingent labor contract. Roman Catholic social thought suggests that it is important to examine rigorously whether forms of social powerlessness lead to a covert coercion that turns seemingly free employment contracts into examples of morally intolerable exploitation.

I am concerned that neither social contract theory nor Roman Catholic social thought will provide fully adequate tools to evaluate the moral acceptability of flexible employment relations, when the employee is a married woman with children. Gender stereotypes might make it appear that female employees choose flexible labor arrangements in order to meet the women's personal preferences to give priority to domestic obligations over workplace opportunities and rewards.

Roman Catholic social thought is particularly vulnerable to a temptation uncritically to endorse women's "choice" of flexible labor relations because the Catholic social tradition is deeply infused with a theory of gender differences as the basis for differential roles for women in the family and, consequently, in the workplace. From the 1890s to the 1930s, Roman Catholic social thought explicitly extolled the patriarchal family as a social institution rooted in God's plan for human persons. The patriarchal family appeared consistent with God's will—as the divine will was revealed through his creation of man and woman with innate, complementary gender traits. Man was made to be the protector and primary breadwinner. Woman was made to be a mother and homemaker. Believing in this set of polar relations—man/breadwinner/public workplace and woman/mother/private home—Leo XIII and Pius XI insisted that justice required that the male worker receive a "living wage," i.e., one sufficient to allow him to support a stay-at-home wife and their children. Pius said pointedly: "Most unfortunate, and to be remedied energetically, is the abuse whereby mothers of families, because of the insufficiency of the father's salary, are forced to engage in gainful occupations outside the domestic walls to the neglect of their own proper [household] cares and duties."[72]

By the 1960s, the patriarchal family as a social model had been quietly dropped by Catholic leaders. During the Second Vatican

Council (1963–65), bishops from around the world hailed a greater recognition of women's social and political rights in a postcolonial world as a sign of moral progress for humanity. In "The Pastoral Constitution on the Church in the Modern World," the bishops declared: "With respect to the fundamental rights of the person, every type of discrimination, whether social or cultural, whether based on *sex,* race, color, social condition, language or religion, is to be overcome and eradicated as contrary to God's intent."[73]

However, in "The Church in the Modern World," the bishops went on to adopt a complex and ultimately unstable position about the role of women in society. Having emphatically affirmed women's equal human rights and having denounced any form of sexual discrimination, the bishops reaffirmed that women had a unique and crucial social role as mothers. The uniqueness of mothers' contributions to the development of children meant that women, while fundamentally equal as human persons, should receive differential treatment from society. The bishops insisted that children, especially younger children, "need the care of their mothers at home." Therefore, society must make special provisions that allow mothers to remain at home with young children. However, consistent with women's right to nondiscrimination "the legitimate social progress of women should not be underrated on that account."[74]

This ambivalent moral stance toward women viewed primarily as mothers is a theme in many of John Paul II's writings. According to him, women are persons with equal human dignity and are entitled to equal consideration in the workplace. However, women are also fundamentally different from men and their participation in the workforce should be structured to facilitate their time-consuming and pivotal role as mothers.

The present pope has come to interpret the moral example of Jesus as characterized by a prophetic equal respect for women. In the letter addressed to the women of the world just prior to the 1995 United Nations Conference on Women in Beijing, China, John Paul II declares, "When it comes to setting women free from every kind of exploitation and domination, the Gospel contains an ever relevant message which goes back to the attitude of Jesus Christ himself."[75] Thus the pope, according to his own understanding of women as both different and equal in human dignity, seeks to find a social pattern that respects the inherent maternal vocation of women while providing them with an equal opportunity to enter into culture, politics, and the marketplace. In the Beijing letter, John Paul II stresses, in particular, an obligation to provide equal pay for equal work, to give women fair consideration for advancement on the job, but still to accommodate women's special needs as mothers.[76] He seems to regard as ideal a social arrangement in which those women who become mothers are guaranteed the financial resources necessary in order to remain at home with their young children. Yet this same ideal society must also guarantee that women have opportunities to participate in the world of work on a basis of total equality with male workers.

From such an official Catholic stance, a period of contingent employment—particularly part-time work—might seem an attractive way to enable women to fulfill their feminine vocation of motherhood while still maintaining their skills as workers. A disproportionate share of women in the peripheral labor force might seem morally unobjectionable if one assumed that contingent jobs provided women greater flexibility to meet family needs. After all, from a gender complementarity perspective, family duties are tasks for which women seem especially well suited and tasks from which women derive special personal fulfillment.

There is an opposite problem with social contract theory. At its root, as applied by Donaldson to business, it seems to ignore gender realities. In Donaldson's original situation of radically individual productivity, there is no indication that producers are sexually differentiated or that they reproduce sexually in a way that places special burdens on the female of the species. Rather, in a fashion typical of social contract thinkers, Donaldson creates an original position in which there is apparently only a collection of self-sufficient adults.

As soon as one introduces babies and toddlers into the original position, then adults have to provide child care services and economic support for those babies and toddlers. Similar services need to be provided for those with severe disabilities, including the frail elderly. If the contractors in the original condition knew that they might be responsible for vulnerable dependents who needed caretaking services, then rational contractors would make demands concerning the relationship of the corporation to the informal care sector. Yet Donaldson never explicitly envisions that workers would want employment arrangements that cohered with responsibilities for dependents.

The only way that the initial contractors could ignore the needs of dependents would be if some other group (exclusive of the contractors) existed who could be expected to handle all caretaking tasks. Several of the great social contract theorists, such as Rousseau, believed that women were precisely such a natural group of caretakers who were not full participants in the social contract. I do not believe that Donaldson and Dunfee make similar assumptions, but they simply do not seriously examine the interface between a public sphere of corporate life and private familial relations.

This is not to suggest that Donaldson is sexually prejudiced. He has consistently named sexually or racially discriminatory business practices as activities that violate minimum norms of justice and, therefore, are absolutely prohibited.[77] One reason that he and Dunfee develop their theory of hypernorms is that they are aware that various cultures have deep-seated practices of subordination of women. Under extant social contracts in some nations, it would be permissible to discriminate against women in hiring and promotion. The hypernorm of equal respect for persons serves as a normative basis to challenge such sexual discrimination.[78]

Still, since Donaldson and Dunfee give limited attention to gender questions when constructing their theoretical position, their theory might not be helpful in evaluating flexible labor contracts for women workers, as long as it seemed that such contracts allowed women voluntarily to satisfy their domestic preferences.

Some pundits do suggest just such a view. They claim that women, who make up a large share of the contingent workforce, choose contingent work precisely because it provides a flexibility that is particularly valuable to women. For example, some commentators assume that the increase in the proportion of the United States workforce that works part-time is a direct result of women's increased participation in the labor force. However, United States government data shows that, since the 1970s, "working women age 25 to 54 have become less likely to be *voluntary* part-time employees."[79] The increase in part-time work over the last twenty-five years does *not* neatly coincide with the appearance of large numbers of new women workers who want part-time jobs. In fact, in the period 1968–87, there was trend to *less voluntary part-time employment* among women.[80] Involuntary part-time work has been rising for the last quarter of a century, primarily to meet the needs of employers, not the needs of workers. Tilly states bluntly that, since about 1970, employers have been "creating [more] part-time jobs even though workers do not want them."[81]

The "flexibility" that contingent work provides is often a more dubious benefit for workers than for employers. A good example in this regard is the flexibility provided to clerical workers who work for temporary help agencies. The company that contacts the temporary help agency specifies how many workers they want, the probable duration of the assignment, the work hours, and the skills needed. The temporary help agency offers a clerical worker a chance to be sent out on an assignment on the terms set forth by the agency's customer.

The "temp"[82] has the flexibility to accept the assignment or reject it. Once she accepts it, she is usually bound by the hours and dates the customer requested. In addition, the counselors at the temporary help agency are interested in filling the customer's request with qualified temps as expeditiously as possible. If a potential temp rejects multiple offers because they don't fit the temp's preferred pattern of days and times, then the counselor is likely to call first other temps who are more "flexible" about accepting assignments. The "choosier" temp may be offered fewer assignments.

We need a specific focus on gender equality in order to analyze adequately the situation of a woman confronted with an offer of employment through a temporary help services agency. Both Roman Catholic social thought and social contract theory as developed in business ethics need a greater sensitivity to patterns of gender exploitation before they can provide an adequate moral analysis of flexible employment contracts offered disproportionately to women workers.

Social Solidarity in a Polarizing Labor Market

Throughout this book, we have seen many examples of a troubling bifurcation of employment opportunities for members of society. The new employability contract may be a good bargain for elite knowledge workers who have the skills to be winners in a competitive, globalized labor market. But the employment security of the large number of workers who lack specialized skills in high demand has been greatly diminished. In *The Work of Nations,* Robert Reich talks about the gulf that is opening up between knowledge workers who are positioned to prosper in a global economy and workers with more mundane skills or few skills at all. Reich asks pointed questions about what will hold communities together and sustain some sense of mutual civic obligation in such an economically polarized situation.[83] As we have seen, Rosabeth Moss Kanter has made similar observations about the diverging life experiences of a cosmopolitan knowledge elite and people with more basic skills whose personal fortunes are bound more tightly to some local economy. Kanter observes that the local and even national ties of the cosmopolitan elite "are weak, although they may feel sentimental attachments to places of their youth or current residence."[84] Sentimental ties are a flimsy moral basis for an obligation to sacrifice immediate self-interest on behalf of the well-being of one's more vulnerable "neighbors."

As we have seen in chapter 4, there are growing economic inequalities among women. A social movement promoting equality for women, coupled with strong growth in professional and managerial jobs, has resulted in economic gains for a relatively small but growing number of women in management and the professions. However, women with a more limited education are struggling to make a living wage, even after some recent increases in the minimum wage. In the face of serious economic inequalities throughout society, it is difficult to see what moral ties will bind members of local communities together.

In a culture such as the United States, where there is a high priority on individualism, this economic polarization creates serious moral dangers. Unless a moral foundation of solidarity is carefully shored up, a social philosophy of liberal individualism will carry the field. Where liberal individualism holds sway, the economically privileged will claim that their affluence is the appropriate reward for their individual creativity, initiative, and hard work. Those with world-class knowledge and skills will acknowledge little moral responsibility or accountability to others in their community who are falling farther behind in an intensifying global economic competition.

The moral stance of "a preferential option for the poor" is only possible if social solidarity is a viable moral prospect. When discussing social solidarity here I find helpful the U.S. Catholic bishops' description of solidarity as "another name for . . . [the] social friendship and civic commitment that make human moral and economic life possible."[85] In other words, human beings are profoundly social beings who achieve their personal fulfillment through relationships with others. Because human beings depend on society for survival and for opportunities to flourish, human beings have a moral obligation to promote the common good. Solidarity is a commitment to the good of the community, which necessarily entails special attention to the needs of the vulnerable members of society.

The Roman Catholic stance of social solidarity, as presented in "Economic Justice for All," involves a view of human motivations quite different from the one assumed in Donaldson's social contract model. I am not claiming that Donaldson might not find the bishops' notion of a social friendship appealing. However, he does not think it is wise to make such assumptions about human solidarity when setting up his crucial original position. In his early arguments, Donaldson simply described people in "the state of individual production" as "ordinary people." By this he meant that these people were not exclusively self-regarding (always seeking their own greatest advantage), but neither were they completely other-regarding (always seeking the well-being of others without regard to their own interests). He also stipulates that people would originally seek to determine whether productive organizations would allow persons more effectively to pursue their economic interests in procuring goods and services.[86] Dunfee and Donaldson report that social contract thinkers rarely assume that the parties setting up the basic social contract are altruistic. One advantage of limiting the original situation to one containing strictly self-interested parties is that any contract accepted by such parties should be plausible to persons with very different sets of motivations— some but not all of which are altruistic.[87]

There is a particular concern for the socially vulnerable in Donaldson's work on the social contract as it applies to business. One prominent source for this concern is Donaldson's use of John Rawls's influential work on social contract thought, *A Theory of*

Justice. Donaldson asserts that the basic social contract must be consistent with fundamental understandings of justice. One aspect of justice that he adopts from Rawls is the assertion that social inequalities are morally acceptable only if, in Donaldson's words, *"they work to the advantage of everyone, including the worst off."*[88] While Donaldson's examples frequently show an empathetic concern with socially disadvantaged groups, such as women confronting sexual discrimination in the workplace or black workers in South Africa during the era of apartheid, solidarity is not a virtue that figures prominently in his theoretical social contract analysis.

As a form of religious ethics, Roman Catholic social thought has a firmer basis on which to call for solidarity as a moral trait that is important in economic situations. The Latin American bishops at Medellín said: "The uniqueness of the Christian message does not so much consist in the affirmation of the necessity for structural change, as it does in the insistence on the conversion of men which will in turn bring about this change."[89] I suggest that one aspect of the conversion that Christianity can inspire is a conversion to solidarity with the socially disadvantaged. In the final chapter, I will explore participation in the eucharist as a source of motivation to act in solidarity with the many workers and their dependents whose employment security has been seriously diminished as a result of the shift to the new employment contract.

6

THE EUCHARIST, SOLIDARITY, AND JUSTICE

*The common table, symbolizing both liberation
and solidarity, stands at the heart and center of the church,
unyielding and insistent, indifferent to the fancies
and fashions of our cultural accommodations, calling us
to conversion . . . and to mission.*[1]

The solidarity symbolized and created at the eucharist—Christianity's common table—is an important wellspring of the struggle for economic justice under conditions of paradoxical prosperity. This chapter will explore the importance for Christian ethics of a eucharist-centered spirituality of justice and solidarity. There is a particular resonance between the eucharist and economic justice because the eucharist is both bodily (materially based) and communal. The eucharist is the sign of divine abundance shared among all the Creator's children.

For some Christian denominations, the eucharist, or Lord's Supper, is *the* central ecclesiastical celebration. Among Roman Catholics, Episcopalians (Anglican Catholics), the Orthodox churches, and some Lutheran churches, the eucharist is celebrated often, and devout members attend at least several times a month. Among other Christian denominations, a service at which preaching is the central activity is more common. Many of these congregations celebrate the eucharist less frequently. Sometimes, it is not part of the main congregational worship service in a typical week. Still, these Christian churches also view this celebration as a key church activity.

The eucharist for Christians, especially for those who celebrate it frequently, is a central part of what ethicist William Spohn calls "lived spirituality." Spohn describes lived spirituality as "the practice of transformative, affective, practical, and holistic disciplines that seek to connect the person with reality's deepest meanings."[2] Spirituality names a set of practices that put human beings in touch with what Paul Tillich names Ultimate Reality. The eucharist is an important part of a set of communal Christian practices that reveal to the Christian community a fundamental moral/theological order of things. One of the deepest truths revealed through a eucharistic spirituality is the interdependence of human beings in and with the Divine Being. As liturgical expert Robert Hovda[3] says, "Liturgy attempts to create a scene, an experience, of that reign of God, divine dominion, the way things are meant to be, *and, at root and in flower, really are.*"[4] A eucharistic foretaste of divine dominion involves a glimpse of a fundamental moral equality among human beings and solidarity between them rooted ultimately in their relationship with the Deity. At the eucharistic table, we come to understand that reality "at root and in flower" is a mystery of benevolent abundance embracing all of humanity and the whole cosmos.

There are vital but insufficiently explored connections between this beneficent reality and our basic moral orientation toward our fellow human beings. Christian spirituality as embodied in the eucharist ought to nourish our passion for justice. Moreover, a eucharistic spirituality ought to provide sustenance for the long journey of the church as a pilgrim people toward greater justice, including greater economic justice.

A eucharistic spirituality of justice and solidarity is particularly powerful because the eucharist is a profoundly embodied reality. At its best, the eucharist touches our sensuous, emotional, and aesthetic selves as well as our ethical selves. Hovda points to the multidimensionality of a eucharistic spirituality when he describes the eucharist as a celebration "in which human dignity is felt (not argued)."[5]

Ethicists need to pay more attention to the impact of the eucharist on the moral formation of the Christian community. This impact is hard to observe and to describe fully. The moral shaping power of the eucharist is profound, especially because it is subtle. As Hovda says, "The common prayer or rite of the Sunday assembly engages and forms us, when we are fully present in it, in ways so basic, so profound, that they steal in upon us, escaping immediate detection."[6]

EUCHARISTIC BREAD AS WORK OF HUMAN HANDS AND JUSTICE

It is particularly appropriate to make connections between the sacrament of the eucharist and economic justice because the elements for the eucharist—bread and wine—are products of human labor. The prayers for the Roman Catholic eucharist acknowledge, for example, that the wine the community offers to the Deity is both a gift of nature—"the fruit of the vine" and the result of human effort—"the work of human hands." Similarly, the prayer recited during the "Preparation of the Gifts" says that bread is something that "earth has given and human hands have made." Liberation theologian Enrique Dussel puts it simply: "Without earth and work there is no bread. Without bread, there is no eucharist."[7]

Thus, the very bread and wine that we offer to the Divine Being and then share with one another reminds us of basic moral truths. Bread and wine require, as raw materials, grain and grapes, which are fruits of the Creator's bounty tended by human hands. As fruits of the earth, bread and wine are a part of that creation intended by the Creator for the sustenance of all the Creator's children.

Bread and wine are also the products of human labor. Grain must be planted, tended, harvested, and processed in order to make bread. Vineyards must be planted, tended, and harvested and the grapes processed in order to make wine. The human labor necessary in order for human beings to have food and drink is a basic sign of both the necessity and the dignity of human labor. In particular, using bread and wine during the eucharist is a sign of the dignity of mundane work that produces ordinary goods to meet fundamental human needs.

During the Offertory section of the Roman Catholic eucharist, the community brings forward the bread and wine that are the fruit of the Creator's benevolence and the work of human hands. The community also collects and brings forward monetary offerings that are used for the support of the parish. In many cases, a portion of the money brought forward is used for charitable purposes.

Disturbingly, liberation theologian Enrique Dussel questions whether Christians who are entangled in systems of economic injustice have economic gifts fit to offer to the Divine Being.

Provocatively, Dussel asks: "Can the fruit stolen from the poor, the oppressed classes, the exploited nations, be offered as eucharistic bread?"[8] Dussel's pointed question reveals that struggling to promote economic justice is fundamental to a Christian community's ability to celebrate the eucharist properly. We ought not join in the equal sharing of bread and wine at Christ's table if we remain indifferent to the distribution of material goods in the larger society. Participating in the eucharist should prod us to examine the economic patterns of our social life.

A EUCHARISTIC SPIRITUALITY AND SOCIAL VISION

Thus, the eucharist should make us more attuned to ethical challenges in our social life. Regular participation in the eucharist sharpens what Spohn calls "our resources of attentiveness." Spohn points out that "prior to thinking clearly about injustice one needs to recognize situations as morally problematic and also notice salient features in them that can lead to change."[9] In our present situation of paradoxical prosperity, it may be difficult for many economically secure Christians to recognize that others suffer serious economic injustices.

Ethicist Bryan Hehir acknowledged this problem when he discussed social justice during an expansionary economic period in the 1980s. He told his audience: "And the difficulty is that in many ways so many other things are so good in the society." He noted that unemployment was then at or below what many economists were calling the "natural" unemployment rate, i.e. an unemployment rate of "five to six percent." In addition, society had experienced "three years of sustained economic growth." Given these positive economic experiences for many, Hehir warned it was hard for ordinary believers to be attentive to the reality that "one out of four children is in poverty" or that "100,000 children go without shelter every night of the week." Hehir cautioned: "You have to work at it to keep that thought [the suffering of poor children] alive."[10] As Hehir was suggesting, the eucharist is one central communal "work" that keeps the thought alive that too many are pushed to the margins of the economy.

It may seem unusual to make a strong connection between spirituality, the eucharist, and economic justice, in part because spirituality may seem an individualistic pursuit. Often people think that spirituality is the individual soul's struggle to achieve a deeper, more satisfying personal relationship with the Deity. To the contrary, as the authors of *God's Fierce Whimsy* say:

> The quest for God, and the concomitant desire to stand open to the power of Spirit, are not in either the first or final place, a private enterprise. Spirituality is fundamentally a communal commitment, a binding between and among, *a relational pilgrimage.*[11]

This type of spirituality recognizes and responds to humanity's inherent sociality. We are relational beings, so we require a relational spirituality.

Only a relational spirituality is adequate for the long struggle to promote justice. Frank Henderson, Kathleen Quinn, and Stephen Larson tell us that along the path toward social justice:

> We will need others with whom to rage and weep over humanity's plight. We will need companions with whom to bear the burdens of social justice. The word "companion" means etymologically "one who eats the same bread." We will need others to share the same bread, most especially the bread of life.[12]

Still, Hovda has an important caution to offer about how the eucharist shapes a Christian perspective on social and economic reform. He declares: "In worship we receive [not a social action blueprint but] something more important—the vision of what we are aiming at."[13] The vision toward which we aim is the Divine Being's inclusive reign of justice and the flourishing of humankind and of all of nature. Indeed, this vision that we aim at challenges the shortcomings of every social or economic blueprint. This realization allows the salutary unity of Christian believers who, in good faith, honestly promote differing economic blueprints as the most effective means of promoting justice. The common themes that the eucharist sets before all members of the church include the moral value of all the beings made by the Creator and the right of all human beings to the material means necessary for a dignified life in community. The eucharist does not present us with a detailed set of policy proposals to address job displacement, contingent employment, economic inequalities, and economic insecurity. It is the duty of participants in the eucharist to join with other persons of good will in their societies to forge such concrete policies to the best of their ability.

The Roman Catholic eucharistic liturgy ends with a sending forth of the believers into the world to make the gospel present in daily life. Reflecting on the eucharist as a memorial of Jesus' Last Supper, theologian David Power says: "Those united in this way cannot approach the ordinary affairs of life expressed in the bread and wine as though they were not bonded in service and eschatological expectation."[14]

EUCHARISTIC SPIRITUALITY, GOSPEL VALUES, AND SOCIAL JUSTICE

A eucharistic spirituality of justice and solidarity has pivotal moral significance because it connects spirituality with several core gospel values. In particular, a eucharistic spirituality taps directly into a proclamation of the Deity's steadfast love for the least powerful, least acceptable members of society. Today, as Christian communities gather around the eucharistic table, they are reenacting the table fellowship that was central to the ministry of Jesus of Nazareth. Joined to that table fellowship, Christians are joined to the eschatological vision that it embodied. Christian table fellowship is a sign of the reign of God/dess. The divine reign is envisioned as an abundant banquet at which all humanity is gathered together and filled with good things.

Jesus of Nazareth was a prophet who had come to proclaim that this reign of God/dess was at hand. The evangelist Luke reflects the importance of the reign of God/dess in the ministry of Jesus when he tells the story of Jesus' initial proclamation of his mission in his home synagogue in Nazareth. Called to read from a scroll containing the words of the prophet Isaiah, Jesus proclaimed the following passage:

> The Spirit of [God] is upon me,
>> because [God] has anointed me
>>> to bring good news to the poor.
> [God] has sent me to proclaim release to the captives
>> and recovery of sight to the blind,
>>> to let the oppressed go free,
> to proclaim the year of [God's] favor.
>> (Luke 4:18–19; Jesus is quoting Isaiah 61:1–2)

Then Jesus declared: "Today this scripture has been fulfilled in your hearing" (Luke 4:21). Thus, Jesus asserted that the objective of his ministry was to proclaim that the reign of God/dess had begun. The redress of economic injustices was a crucial aspect of that reign. The Spirit sent Jesus to proclaim good news to the poor.

In addition, according to some scripture scholars, Jesus announced a jubilee year. A jubilee year was a Hebrew institution that sought to promote ecological responsibility and economic equity. Every fifty years, the land was to be allowed to remain fallow. Members of the Hebrew community who had sold themselves into indentured servitude were to be freed. The Hebrew community was to redistribute farmland—the basic economic asset—among all families in the community. Yahweh commands this redistribution of land because "the land is mine; with me you are but aliens and tenants" (Leviticus 25:23). Thus, in what Luke presents as Jesus' first sermon, Jesus stresses the Spirit's concern for the poor and for economic equity as a communal characteristic.

Jesus proclaimed the reign of God/dess through his actions as well as his words. He practiced a table fellowship with social outcasts that was a foretaste of the reign of God/dess. Properly observant forms of table fellowship were critical questions for several other Jewish groups in Judea and Galilee during the time of Jesus. Both the Essenes and the Pharisees stressed cultically pure forms of table fellowship—the Essenes among their inner circle at Qumran and the Pharisees in the midst of everyday life. Indeed, according to L. William Countryman, the Pharisees who were the contemporaries of Jesus "seem to have concentrated their attention on issues of table fellowship. They undertook to eat their ordinary meals in the state of purity that Leviticus demanded only of the priestly families. . . . This commitment required constant vigilance against contracting uncleanness."[15] In contrast, Jesus did not allow a preoccupation with cultic purity to separate him from society's outcasts. He is said to have eaten with sinners, prostitutes, and tax collectors.

Scripture scholar Kathleen Corley suggests that we should not accept unquestioningly the description of the women who shared Jesus' table as "prostitutes." This biblical scholar says that a denunciation of the character and purity of the women who ate with Jesus might well be a reflection of broader social controversies concerning which public roles ought to be assumed by women. She points out that this was an era in the history of the Roman Empire in which women were taking a larger role in public events. Corley continues: "This social innovation was the result of larger economic changes and fluctuations in the market economy which placed economic and social power in the hands of women."[16] She shows that enemies of a variety of social groups accused those groups of holding banquets at which "promiscuous" women were present.[17] Therefore, the accusation that Jesus dined with prostitutes may have been a stereotypical slur.

Nonetheless, Jesus' offer of table fellowship to women definitely dismayed some of his contemporaries. In the Gospels, particularly Matthew's Gospel, women whose behavior invited social scorn were welcomed as the Jesus community joined in a meal that prefigured the eschatological banquet. Corley points out that in Matthew's Gospel, the heavenly banquet is likened to *a marriage feast*—a type of celebration at which women and children were customarily present even in socially conservative families.[18] Indeed, Elisabeth Schüssler Fiorenza proclaims that "the central symbolic actualization of the *basileia* vision of Jesus is not the cultic meal but the festive table of a royal banquet or wedding feast."[19]

However, according to the parables, this was a surprising sort of royal banquet or wedding feast. The guests were not solely those who strictly observed the Torah requirements for purity— behavior befitting those who ate at a priestly table. Nor were the guests only the wealthy and influential persons who would usually have been invited to a royal banquet or a well-to-do family's wedding feast. Rather, in the parables the guests invited to the eschatological banquet are sinners, the poor, and other social outcasts (Matthew 22:1–10; Luke 14:16–24).

Schüssler Fiorenza also points out that many tax collectors and prostitutes, including some who feasted with Jesus, were probably individuals in desperate economic circumstances. Their economic options were so limited that they were forced to engage in socially despised activities in order to obtain money. Thus, Jesus offered table fellowship to people who were disgraced as a result of socioeconomic patterns that marginalized them.[20]

Jesus' practice of table fellowship and some of his parables about feasts set before the poor underline the importance for Christians of the virtue of solidarity across economic divisions. Perhaps the most dramatic such parable is the story of the rich man and the beggar, Lazarus, found in Luke 16:19–27. Lazarus was the ill beggar who lay starving just outside the gate of the rich man's home. Yet, the rich man made no effort to feed Lazarus. Indeed, the rich man did not even offer the scraps from his sumptuous table to the ill, homeless man. Then, both men died. Lazarus found his reward in paradise alongside Abraham. At the same time, the rich man suffered eternal torment in the flames of hell because of his callous indifference to Lazarus's suffering and need.

Pope Paul VI drew upon this parable to urge solidarity with the economically deprived. In *Populorum Progressio,* Paul VI spoke of a duty of human solidarity that requires that the economically privileged show "great generosity, much sacrifice and unceasing effort" on behalf of the world's poor. Only such a continuing practice of solidarity could open up the new possibility that "the poor man Lazarus" could "sit down at the same table with the rich man."[21] Solidarity could open up the possibility of genuine eucharistic community among rich and poor—community supported by the ongoing struggle for economic justice.

A similar connection between eucharistic spirituality and solidarity with the economically disadvantaged is found in the work of John Paul II. Ethicist Drew Christiansen indicates that,

> like Paul VI before him, John Paul takes table fellowship to be the root metaphor for a Catholic conception of justice. He argues for "each people's right to be seated at the table of the common banquet" . . . and interprets the lack of North-South collaboration in development as re-enacting the indifference of the rich man to Lazarus.[22]

Through the eucharist, present-day Christian communities live out a connection not only to the parables and the practice of table fellowship during the ministry of Jesus, but also to the practices of the earliest community of believers in Jerusalem who gathered together after the death, resurrection, and ascension of Jesus. Dussel imagines that the original Christian community (described in Acts 2:44–46) actually achieved a eucharistic unity that was both sacramental and eschatological. Acts 2:44–46 describes the earliest converts of Peter in Jerusalem as having sold all their property, distributing the proceeds on the basis of need, and meeting to "break bread" in daily communal meals. Thus, Dussel understands that some of the wealthier people among the earliest followers of Jesus shared all they had so that the poorest members of the community would no longer lack basic material goods. As Dussel envisions it, "The eucharistic bread of those 'whose faith had drawn them together' was bread that had satisfied *need*, in justice" through a general distribution of the community's joint possessions for the sake of the destitute. Dussel imagines a community that experienced, in its communal meals,

> the joy of consuming, of eating, of satisfaction. It was a bread of life, of the community, of love. . . . it is the horizon of critical understanding of every economic system in history; justice as the *practical condition* which *makes possible* the eucharistic celebration which saves.[23]

Dussel relies on an idealized portrait of the early community of Christians in Jerusalem. There is evidence, even in Acts itself (Acts 5:1–11), that the situation was more complex than Dussel recounts. Converts were *not required* to sell their property or to give *all* proceeds from the sale of any tangible property to the leaders of the community as a condition of participation (Acts 5:4). Moreover, not all new members were prepared to live up to the communal ideal of economic sharing. The author of Acts tells the story of a wealthy husband and wife who sought to retain a portion of the funds gained from the sale of land. While Ananias and Sapphira were struck dead by the Deity, their misdeeds included lying to Peter and the community about the proceeds of the land deal and, more importantly, a lack of faith in the proximate return of Jesus. They were not struck down solely for retaining some money for their personal use.

Wealthier members of the Jerusalem community probably sold their property with the expectation that Jesus, the Son of Man, would soon return at the head of a band of angels, end earthly existence as humanity had known it, and initiate the heavenly reign of God/dess. Generously divesting oneself of one's earthly assets for the sake of the poor might have been somewhat easier for persons who believed that earthly treasures would not long retain their value anyway. When Ananias and Sapphira hoarded some of the proceeds from their land deal, the couple was showing doubt about a proximate return of God in glory.

At the dawn of the twenty-first century, the eucharist connects us to the earliest Christians, and it challenges us as it challenged them to transform our lives in light of the good news that the reign of God/dess is at hand. Indeed, Hovda says: "It is liturgy's actualization of the reign of God, the heavenly banquet, that invites us to permanent dissatisfaction, repentance and growth."[24] One important form of dissatisfaction that eucharistic fellowship should stir up in our hearts and minds is a dissatisfaction with the growing economic inequality—inequality among women as well as among men—that is a global characteristic of postindustrial capitalism.

BETRAYAL OF THE EUCHARISTIC VISION AROUND THE CHURCH'S TABLE

The church is a pilgrim people, on the way toward the reign of God/dess, but never "there" yet. The church is also a sinful people who betray the vision of human solidarity and human fulfillment that is embodied in the eucharist. This was a truth that Robert Hovda recognized bluntly. He declared: "The church is not only a community of sinners, but also a sinful community."[25] In other words, the church itself is also always immersed in sin as it gathers at the eucharistic table. Theologian Mary Catherine Hilkert concurs: "A fundamental tension remains within the celebration of every Christian assembly, since the gathered community and its institutional structures are marked by sin as well as grace."[26]

Indeed, in his prophetic critique of the corruption of the Christian sacraments, Latin American liberation theologian Juan Segundo denounced the failure of many eucharistic celebrations to create genuine community. He charged: "In the celebrations with which we are familiar, the Eucharist brings people next to each other; it juxtaposes them. It does not make a community out of the participants."[27] This criticism is echoed by Hovda, who declares: "Nothing is more inimical to the kind of Sunday assembly we now desire than the lack of solidarity, the obvious way we gather as lone consumers in a vast spiritual enterprise."[28] In particular, Segundo charged that too many eucharists fail to inspire the participants to care about or to act on behalf of justice for the poorest and the most vulnerable members of the assembly.

Ethicist Margaret Farley turned her penetrating gaze on Christian liturgical life and found moral difficulties that cry out for serious ethical analysis. Farley frankly admitted that when Christian believers meet together for worship on the contemporary scene, "The human spirit is as often dulled, distracted, burdened, as it is touched and awakened, freed in faith and hope. Far from 'building up' the Body of Christ, common worship often paralyzes it." She continued: "Liturgical experience, to a great extent, is not one of opening to the presence of God among us, nor does it form in us dispositions of love in relation to our neighbor. Indeed, the life of faith may be limited, choked off, by our seeming inability to find life in our common worship."[29]

Farley pointedly named a central moral problem in the worship life of the community of believers. She decried the church's "failure . . . to translate into its own life and structures the very norms of justice which it proclaims prophetically to the world."[30] She asserted that when liturgical practices themselves violate justice, the worship life of many believers suffers. I would add that, under such circumstances, the power of the liturgy to shape believers' moral perceptions, attitudes, and actions also suffers.

THE EQUALITY OF WOMEN AT THE EUCHARISTIC TABLE

There is a painful irony, for me, in trying to write about the eucharist as a feminist Roman Catholic ethicist. The current Vatican statement that ratifies the long-standing practice of excluding women from the role of presider at the eucharist[31] is experienced by many women (and men) as an insult to the human dignity of women and to their equal worth as persons and as beings made in the image of the Deity.

Gathering around the eucharistic table, women and men who are committed to gender equality receive a deeply disturbing double message. On the one hand, members of the community are all equal in a profound and fundamental way as they gather to share the eucharistic bread and wine. On the other hand, in the Roman Catholic Church, only ordained males are allowed to preside at the eucharist, proclaiming the word of God/dess in the homily and consecrating the bread and wine on behalf of the assembly. The exclusion of women from the ministerial priesthood, and consequently from the role of celebrant at the eucharist, creates an impression of male superiority that is antithetical to gender equality.

Indeed, in the history of the church, an exclusively male priesthood was frequently justified by assertions that women, as a sex, were socially and ontologically inferior and, therefore, could not appropriately serve as mediators between God and humanity. Only socially and ontologically superior men could convincingly represent Christ to the community. For example, Thomas Aquinas said: "Since it is not possible in the female sex to signify eminence of degree, for woman is in the state of subjection, it follows that she cannot receive the sacrament of Orders."[32]

In the twentieth century, faced with the rise of gender equality as a powerful moral norm in secular society, the officials of the Roman Catholic Church have changed their rationale for excluding women from the priesthood, but they adamantly defend the continuing practice of excluding women from consideration for ordination. Indeed, John Paul II has emphatically declared that exclusion of women from the priesthood is not a sign that women have less human worth. He has insisted that this practice should not be judged to be an example of morally repugnant sexual discrimination.[33] Still, Roman Catholic authorities take the position that the church cannot ordain women to the ministerial priesthood *and* remain faithful to the will of God, revealed through the actions of Jesus, who selected only male apostles. Thus, the present official stance is that God wills separate roles for women and men in the eucharistic assembly (and elsewhere in the life of the church).

Church leaders are not able presently to provide a clear theological explanation for this exclusionary church practice. The principal remaining official explanation for the exclusion of women from the priesthood is that men and women have been created with fundamental sexual differences that are consistent with different ecclesiastical roles. These differences allow the sexes to complement one another and, hence, to enrich life in society and the church. Church leaders have not fully elaborated this theory of sexual complementarity.

John Paul II, who is a strong advocate of this position, has described women as having a maternal nature that makes them uniquely sensitive to new life and especially willing to care for children and others in need of help. He describes women as having a loving nature that manifests itself in special compassion for the socially vulnerable. Under basic understandings of justice, it is fair to assign different roles to different persons or groups *if, and only if,* the unique characteristics of those persons or groups make them particularly suited to the roles in question. It is fair to exclude others from certain positions if they permanently lack certain abilities essential to the performance of the role. However, none the qualities that John Paul II has described as essential to women by virtue of their female nature is a characteristic that makes women incapable of being competent priests.

So, the only way to defend the exclusion of women from consideration for ordination is to say that it represents the *inscrutable* will of God, made known through Jesus' selection of only men among the Twelve (apostles). This position opens up a troubling gulf between human justice and God's ultimately arbitrary will. As a religious ethicist, I am deeply disturbed by the claim that God's justice and human justice are sharply different when the issue is equality for women.

At present, when women and men who are committed to gender equality assemble for the eucharist, they confront the contradictory reality of a eucharist banquet that is both a foretaste of the reign of God/dess and a sacramental meal at which women are not fully equal. As I have emphasized in this chapter, it is one function of the eucharist to make us dissatisfied with any practices in the world (including the economy) or the church that insult human dignity. For many of us, the exclusion of women, because they are women, from the role of eucharistic celebrant is such a practice.

RACIAL SEGREGATION IN EUCHARISTIC ASSEMBLIES

Discrimination against women in leadership roles at the eucharist is not the only sign of sin in the eucharistic practices of Christian churches. For example, there is also a long history of racial discrimination at the eucharistic table in the United States. In this chapter, I will draw examples from the history of the Christian denomination that I know best, the Roman Catholic Church. However, the history of other Christian denominations in the United States contains similar legacies of racial supremacy, racial prejudice, and racial separation.

African Americans have frequently been denied a position of equal dignity during eucharistic celebrations in Catholic communities in the United States. For example, in Louisiana during the antebellum period, the ideology of white racial superiority led prominent white lay Catholics to insist on the following order in which parishioners would approach the communion rail: Whites should receive first, then free persons of color, and last slaves (who had their masters' permission).[34] Even after emancipation, black Catholics were frequently restricted to less desirable seats in the rear or the balconies of Catholic churches. The practice of distributing communion to blacks only after all whites had come forward continued in many places.

The Roman Catholic Church in the United States began to face an even greater challenge when African Americans moved to northern cities in large numbers in the late nineteenth century. This northern migration of African Americans continued through the first half of the twentieth century. Historian Jay P. Dolan indicates: "The immigrant church [of the nineteenth and early twentieth century] was clearly a white people's church, and few blacks found a home there; those that did were clearly third-class citizens."[35]

Racially segregated parishes in northern cities were in part an unintentional consequence of the Catholic policy of establishing ethnic parishes to serve a linguistically and culturally diverse population of immigrants from Europe. Well into the twentieth century, northern cities had German parishes, Irish parishes, Italian parishes, and Polish parishes. In fact, some of those parishes continue to exist in large cities even today.

So in one sense, it was standard practice to organize an African American parish and to encourage all African American Catholics to attend that church. However, it was also true that racially segregated parishes were a comfortable arrangement for many racially prejudiced, European American, Catholic clergy and laity. For example, during the nineteenth century, the diocese of Chicago had an explicit policy prohibiting African American Catholics from being registered as parishioners in European American parishes.[36] After World War II, when the burgeoning white Catholic middle class flocked to the suburbs, de facto racial segregation in suburban neighborhoods in the North meant that many Catholic parishes organized along geographical lines remained overwhelmingly white.

However, the history of the relationship between white and black Catholics is a complex one. Some white Catholics have been quite willing to share the eucharistic table with blacks. For example, the first African American Catholic priest, Augustus Tolton, was the pastor of a small African American parish in Illinois. Other local pastors became jealous when many white Catholics from nearby parishes began receiving the sacraments from "the nigger priest." Tolton magnanimously described the ordinary white Catholics of Quincy, Illinois, as "good-hearted, charitable, and non-prejudicial, [harboring] no feelings of bitterness at all against a man on account of complexion."[37] (The same could not be said of local white clergy.)

Accommodation to white racism and an ideology of white supremacy was never the whole story. Repeatedly, African American Catholics publicly challenged racist church practices and policies. A small group of European American clergy and laity were allies in the struggle. For example, the Catholic Interracial Council under the tutorship of John LaFarge and the Friendship House movement under Catherine de Hueck promoted racial justice in many cities.

Still, the history of racism within the Roman Catholic Church in the United States has created a legacy of racial discrimination and racial separation that has left an enduring mark on our eucharistic celebrations. Ethicist Kenneth Himes has honestly and courageously acknowledged that "our worshiping communities too often reflect rather than challenge the *de facto* apartheid of our nation."[38]

EUCHARISTS CELEBRATED BETWEEN "BROKENNESS" AND "WHOLENESS"

The Christian community continues to be immersed in the sin of the world and that sin, unacknowledged and unrepented, taints our eucharists. In the 1970s, the liberation theologian Juan Segundo decried a crisis in the Christian sacraments. He diagnosed that crisis as one rooted specifically in believers' failure to recognize and repent of the social sins in their daily lives when those believers gathered for the eucharist. Segundo offered an example in which economic injustice, compounded by a lack of compassion and a smug hypocrisy, marred the Christian unity of the eucharist. He decried the evil done when churches condemned and excluded women—abandoned by their husbands—who lived in illicit unions with other men. Segundo recognized that these women were desperate for male support while raising their children, because a poor or working-class woman could not "care for the needs of her family by herself . . . because woman's work is not priced in those terms." Segundo regretted that such a woman was considered by many Christians, including many clergy, as unfit to be a full participant in the eucharist. Why should she be excluded from the church when "continuing participation in that community is afforded to those who help to keep this societal structure [i.e., the economic marginalization of poor women] going—by their sins of omission at the very least"?[39]

Still, the eucharist itself challenges Christian believers to recognize, confess, and repent of just such moral failures and to call upon divine grace as a source for moral transformation. As Hovda declares:

> All believing communities are miserable signs of a reign of God that explodes into our scene when we assemble on Sunday and both liberates and reconciles all of God's created variety, not in competition but in harmony, not as higher or lower but as equals . . . as testament to the wondrous and multiform beauty of a human race, finally, with God's grace beginning to understand itself.[40]

Divine grace makes our eucharists sacraments—signs that bring about unity among humans, unity with the rest of creation, and unity with the Deity that they signify.

Theologian David Power reminds us of the moral significance of the sacrament of the eucharist: "So it is that church gatherings are faced by their [eucharistic] ritual with issues of human need and human justice. The eschatological promise of the rule of God, though it transcends our concepts of time, is tied to the hope of a covenant justice here on earth."[41]

A tension between "eschatological vision and experiential reality," between "wholeness and brokenness," is manifest in both Jesus' proclamation of the reign of God/dess and our eucharists.[42] Schüssler Fiorenza speaks of Jesus' ministry as "the mediation of God's future into the structures and experiences of his own time and people."[43] In the eucharist, we continue that mediation in our times in memory of Jesus. Our mediation is not complete or coherent unless it leads us to solidarity with economic "outcasts" in the global labor market.

EUCHARIST-CENTERED SOLIDARITY AND THE NEW JOB CONTRACT

A eucharist-centered spirituality of solidarity and justice is an important moral resource in an economic context in which people could be pressured to accept a form of "employability" that threatens to degenerate into a morally destructive individualism. On the surface, the concept of employability might appear to emphasize that wage laborers are *each* responsible, first and foremost, for directing their *individual* careers, always looking for an opportunity to enhance their *personal* "employability" profile.

In particular, overtones of individualism in the employability model might seem to justify wide economic inequalities. An individualistic interpretation of employability might appear to excuse the economically privileged from an obligation to be in solidarity with those with fewer marketable economic skills or those who become displaced from their jobs in a turbulent labor market. Under an employability paradigm, members of the global knowledge/managerial elites could easily interpret their privileged economic position as simply a fair reward for their top skills and their astute management of their personal careers.

While the majority of the global knowledge/managerial elites are men, a growing group of women could adopt this same ideology. These women could interpret their significant economic gains as fair rewards for their skills, savvy, and tenacity. In fact, to the extent that many of these women may have faced sexual discrimination during their careers, such women might be even more tempted to interpret their success as a hard-won personal achievement.

Dussel's insight that the communal meals of the Christian community have the potential to serve as a "horizon of critical understanding of every economic system" is crucial here.[44] A eucharistic spirituality ought to sharpen awareness among Christians of the darker underside of the dynamic United States economy. Regular participation in the eucharist—with an openness to the values that it embodies—should create and strengthen in worshipers a sense of the connectedness among human beings, with the whole created world, and with the Creator/Redeemer.

This sense of connectedness ought to make Christians attentive to the *communal* dimension of any humane employability contract. The eucharistic spirituality that I have been discussing in this chapter is congruent with an appreciation of the social responsibility of capital found in Roman Catholic social thought. It resonates with the Catholic teaching about a "social mortgage" on capital, which was discussed in chapter 5 of this book.

If the employability model is to become the new social contract for jobs in the United States, then the obligations of employers toward *all* their workers need to be closely examined. Corporate training becomes a key issue under an employability contract, so it would be imperative to see that appropriate training is available to all employees. Persons displaying the virtue of solidarity would be particularly concerned to see that socially disadvantaged workers got a fair share of training opportunities. This would require the opposite of present training patterns in which the majority of the corporate-sponsored training opportunities go to white male workers who are already relatively well educated.

Viewing the question of employability from the perspective of a eucharist-based spirituality of solidarity and justice would require facing squarely the central difficulty with that model under current conditions of global capitalism. Some of the key opportunities to develop and to hone skills that workers need represent a risky investment on the employer's part. The whole notion of employability means that workers need to develop skills that are valuable in the *external* labor market. In particular, workers with limited, firm-specific skills need an opportunity to develop general skills such as basic computer literacy or problem-solving skills. However, some workers who gain such skills at company expense will leave to work somewhere else, possibly even for a competitor.

The idea of increasing employability during a short-term employment relationship might make sense in a few cases. These would be situations where highly skilled technical, professional, or managerial workers apply the skills they bring with them to a specific corporate project. The workers enhance their skills in the process of working on a cutting-edge project and, when the project is over, the now even more skilled workers move on to other projects with different employers. However, for most workers, whose skills are more mundane, a workable employability contract would require corporate investment in training. In a situation where worker tenure is uncertain, it is difficult to justify that corporate investment on financial grounds.

Thus, there is an irony at the heart of the employability model. The current employer may not be able to capture an economic return on the employer's investment in the employee's skills, unless the employer can retain the employee for a significant time after training. While the employability contract excludes a promise of long-term employment, the ironic solution to this dilemma appears to be a commitment by top management to promote a long-term employment relationship with a skillful workforce. In other words, top executives would have to make it a key corporate aim (alongside competitiveness and profitability) to create a steady stream of productive work for employees who had been enhancing their skills. This scenario means that employers would actually provide that employment security which the employability model explicitly disavows.

There is another problem with the employability model. Many contingent workers, particularly temporary workers, do not fit well within an employability model. After all, one key attraction for a corporation in the use of contingent workers is that it reduces the number of "real" employees to whom the corporation has legal and moral responsibilities, including its responsibilities to assist in the skill development that is at the core of the employability contract. It is particularly disturbing that many large companies have fired employees only to bring them back on an insecure contract worker basis. Even part-time workers who remain with a company for a longer period are less likely to receive corporate-sponsored training. If workers and their families are now to derive economic security by remaining highly "employable" *over the span of a normal career,* then special attention needs to be given to the situation of contingent workers. A spirituality of solidarity and justice would entail a special concern for the marginalization of those contingent workers who may be excluded from corporate-sponsored programs to increase employees' skills.

A eucharist-based solidarity should also make Christians more sensitive to the role that society plays in sustaining worker employability and, with it, economic security. In the first place, the knowledge and skills that are increasingly the source of individual and familial economic security are not solely an individual achievement. Rather, they are the fruit of a socially shared stock of knowledge. The employability of an individual worker is based on a social history of education (broadly understood). For this reason, questions concerning educational equity are crucial questions related to economic justice in society.

In the second place, in a turbulent labor market where many jobs are being destroyed—even when unemployment rates are low and net job growth is strong—the United States government must provide greater support to assist workers who suffer serious harm when they lose their jobs. A religiously based sense of solidarity that extends to one's neighbors in the civic community is one important source for a sense that one has a moral obligation to assist fellow citizens who are losing out in this turbulent labor market.

Examining the prospects of the knowledge/managerial elite who operate on a global scale, Robert Reich has asked: "What do we owe one another as members of the same society who no longer inhabit the same economy?"[45] He goes on to acknowledge that the answer to that question will depend on whether the knowledge/managerial elite continue to be tied by bonds of communal responsibility, what the Catholic bishops have called "social friendship,"[46] to other persons in society. I suggest that a sense of solidarity fostered around the eucharistic table is one (but only one) moral resource pressing us to take Reich's question seriously. A eucharistic-based solidarity also supplies one answer to the question why managerial and professional women ought to care about the plight of women with less formal education who are struggling in insecure, low-paying service jobs.

Emphatically, I am not suggesting some version of the argument that all would be right with the United States if we could make it a "Christian nation." I am proposing a eucharistic spirituality as one useful element in the moral experience of Christians as a particular religious group. Other religious groups have their own specific religious experiences that give rise to other particular sources of concern for the well-being of one's neighbors. In addition, many persons who have no religious commitments also develop a strong sense of moral obligation to others who belong to the community. For example, using a philosophic social contract approach, Thomas Donaldson articulates an obligation (under the norm of justice) to ensure that corporate practices do not harm the more vulnerable members of society.[47] A eucharist-based sense of solidarity is *one, but only one,* source of motivation for persons to accept obligations to help other members of the community who are at risk in a turbulent labor market.

In times of general prosperity and economic growth, a eucharist-centered spirituality of solidarity and justice prods Christians to ask whether the new job contract provides a basis for economic well-being for workers and their families that is *sustainable over time*. Trust that one will have continuing access to the economic resources necessary for a dignified life in community in the future is the core element in economic security as a human good. There are serious questions about whether the new job contract does provide economic security and if so, for whom.

When big corporations continue to dismiss large numbers of workers in order to keep corporate profits high, keeping one's job becomes a gamble. Many hard-working, loyal employees with decent skills are let go because firing them improves the corporation's bottom line. Under such circumstances, losing one's job is like holding a losing ticket in some random economic lottery. In this dynamic economy, serious economic penalties are paid disproportionately by those displaced workers who cannot readily find another good job. For example, men or women in their fifties or early sixties who are fired from jobs that offered good pay and benefits may have a very difficult time finding comparable jobs elsewhere. But these workers don't "deserve" to suffer such losses.

Throughout much of the 1990s, the turbulence in the United States labor market created anxiety for most American wage laborers and their families. Seven years into an economic expansion, with wages finally beginning to increase in real terms and with a tight labor market, many people are starting to feel a bit more confident about their economic futures. Soothed by positive economic news, especially the creation of an amazing number of jobs, some workers are beginning to say, "I may be let go by my company tomorrow, but there are plenty of other jobs out there. I'll get another good job right away." However, during the next recession—and there will be a next recession—under the employability contract employers will be free to fire even long-time employees quickly, and it will be hard for many displaced workers to find other good jobs.

There is much to applaud in this dynamic United States economy, which has created a very large number of new jobs for persons who need them. Many economic commentators believe that labor flexibility (which is a key reason to move to the employability contract) is a necessary element in an economy capable of creating many jobs. Still, there are open questions about the human harms suffered because of our dynamic economy, including a reduction of economic security for many workers and their families. Robert Hovda understood the eucharist as an experience that always left the Christian community dissatisfied with the harm and injustice in any economic system. He declared: "No matter how much . . . progress we make, the reign of God [toward which the eucharist points] will always stand in judgment over every new political and economic structure, as over the old—criticizing, goading, inviting and inspiring."[48] The eucharist prods Christians to join with other persons of good will to insist that any new job contract is acceptable only if it really provides economic security for workers and their families.

Notes

Introduction

1. U.S. Department of Labor, Bureau of Labor Statistics, "The Employment Situation," USDL 98-91, March 6, 1998, table 2 (http://www.bls.gov).

1. A Loss of Employment Security

1. "The Politics of Unemployment: Europe Hits a Brick Wall," *The Economist*, April 5, 1997, 21.

2. Nathaniel C. Nash, "In Germany, Downsizing Means 10.3% Jobless," *New York Times*, March 7, 1996, D1, D6.

3. AMA Research, *1996 Survey on Downsizing, Job Elimination, and Job Creation* (New York: American Management Association, 1996), 8.

4. Mark N. Vamos, ed., "America, Land of the Shaken," *Business Week*, March 11, 1996, 65.

5. Louis Uchitelle, "Job Insecurity of Workers Is a Big Factor in Fed Policy," *New York Times*, February 27, 1997, D6. The same survey data provides the basis for Michael Mandel, "Workers Have a Case of Nerves, but Job Jitters May Be Leveling Off," *Business Week*, September 16, 1996, 30.

6. Robert D. Hershey Jr., "Labor Market Tightens but Pay Gains Stay Slim," *New York Times*, September 5, 1996, D4.

7. AMA Research, *1996 Survey on Downsizing*, 8.

8. Steven Davis, John Haltiwanger, and Scott Schuh, *Job Creation and Destruction* (Cambridge: MIT Press, 1996), 18.

9. Ibid., 37, 45.

10. Ibid., 18, footnote 2.

11. Ibid., 20.

12. Ibid.

13. Ibid., 123.

14. Ibid., 121.

15. Gene Koretz, "Economic Trends: Job Mobility, American-Style," *Business Week,* January 27, 1997, 20.

16. Henry S. Farber, *Are Lifetime Jobs Disappearing? Job Duration in the United States: 1973–1993,* National Bureau of Economic Research, Working Paper no. 5014, February 1995, 15.

17. "The State of Working America, 1996–97: Executive Summary" (Washington, D.C.: Economic Policy Institute, 1996) (http://www.epn.org/epi/epswa-ex.html).

18. Farber, *Are Lifetime Jobs Disappearing?* 26.

19. U.S. Department of Labor, Bureau of Labor Statistics, "Employee Tenure in the Mid-1990s," USDL 97-25 (http://stats.bls.gov:80/newsrels.htm).

20. Ibid.

21. Ibid., table 3.

22. Ibid.

23. Farber, *The Changing Face of Job Loss in the United States: 1981–1993,* National Bureau of Economic Research, Working Paper no. 5596, 13. "Secular" is a technical term that indicates that there is an underlying trend in a certain direction despite variations over the course of the business cycle. In this case, Farber is suggesting that there is early evidence of a long-term decline in job security.

24. AMA Research, *1996 Survey on Downsizing,* 2.

25. Ibid., 8.

26. Steve Lohr, "Though Upbeat on the Economy, People Still Fear for Their Jobs," *New York Times,* December 29, 1996, 1.

27. American Management Association, *1997 AMA Survey: Corporate Job Creation, Job Elimination, and Downsizing: Summary of Key Findings* (New York: American Management Association, 1997), 1.

28. This is not to say that companies have not sometimes found it necessary to restore some of the jobs that were "abolished" during ill-conceived waves of downsizing. Many observers report that some companies downsized without enough attention to core business functions. They often instituted across-the-board job cuts that left them without sufficient staff to handle crucial corporate activities effectively. After a period of disruption, some employers were forced to restore some of these jobs.

29. AMA Research, *1996 Survey on Downsizing,* 3. However, automation is also a reason why companies hire new workers who have the skills necessary to install, maintain, and operate automated systems. In 1996, 9 percent of companies hired workers because of automation, while 10 percent of firms fired workers as a result of automation. *1996 Survey on Downsizing,* 6.

30. American Management Association, "Corporate Downsizing, Job Elimination, and Job Creation: Summary of Key Findings" (New York: American Management Association, 1996), 7.

31. U.S. Department of Labor, Bureau of Labor Statistics. "Worker Displacement during the Early 1990s," USDL 94-434, September 14, 1994 (http://stats.bls.gov/news.release/disp.toc.htm).

32. John Cassidy, "All Worked Up: Is Downsizing Really New or Is It Just Business as Usual?" *The New Yorker,* April 22, 1996, 53.

33. Farber, *Changing Face of Job Loss,* 15.

34. Michael J. Mandel, "Economic Anxiety," *Business Week,* March 11, 1996, 50.

35. Farber, *Changing Face of Job Loss,* 15.

36. Ibid., 16.

37. Ibid., 22–23.

38. Ibid., 20, 22.

39. U.S. Department of Labor, Bureau of Labor Statistics, "Women in the Workforce: An Overview," Report 892, July 1995, 18.

40. Farber, *Changing Face of Job Loss,* 26.

41. U.S. Department of Labor, "Women in the Workforce, 16.

42. U.S. Department of Labor, Bureau of Labor Statistics, "Worker Displacement during the Mid-1990s," USDL 96-446, October 25, 1996 (http://stats.bls.gov/pub/news.release/disp.txt).

43. "The State of Working America, 1996–97: Executive Summary."

44. Farber, *Changing Face of Job Loss,* 29.

45. Adam Seitchik, "Who Are Displaced Workers?" in *Job Displacement: Consequences and Implications for Policy,* ed. John T. Addison (Detroit: Wayne State University Press, 1991), 76.

46. Farber, *Are Lifetime Jobs Disappearing?* 11.

47. U.S. Department of Labor, Bureau of Labor Statistics, "Employee Tenure in the Mid-1990s," USDL 97-25, January 30, 1997 (http://stats.bls.gov:80/newsrels.htm). However, median job tenure would be expected to decline in 1996, since a group of older men who had been out of the labor market moved back into new jobs starting in 1995. A growing number of older men in new jobs (and hence with very low job tenure) would lower the median job tenure figure.

48. Koretz, "Economic Trends," 20.

49. Cassidy, "All Worked Up," 53.

50. Farber, *Changing Face of Job Loss,* 14.

51. Ibid., 23.

52. Joseph Nocera, "Living with Layoffs," *Fortune,* April 1, 1996, 71.

53. U.S. Department of Labor, Bureau of Labor Statistics, "Worker Displacement during the Mid-1990s," USDL 96-446.

54. Farber, *Changing Face of Job Loss,* 26.

55. Louis Uchitelle, "Six Years in the Plus Column for the U.S. Economy," *New York Times,* March 12, 1997, D4.

56. U.S. Department of Labor, Bureau of Labor Statistics. "Worker Displacement during the Early 1990s," USDL 94-434.

57. U.S. Department of Labor, Bureau of Labor Statistics. "Worker Displacement during the Mid-1990s," USDL 96-446.

58. Jocelyn Gutchess, "International Comparison of Employment Adjustments," in *Employment Security and Labor Market Flexibility: An International Perspective,* ed. Kazutoshi Koshiro (Detroit: Wayne State University Press, 1992), 210.

59. This was particularly important to the White House since it exceeded the 8 million net new jobs that Bill Clinton had promised to create during his 1992 presidential election campaign. "Press Briefing by Secretary of the Treasury Robert Rubin, Secretary of Labor Robert Reich, National Economic Advisor Dr. Laura Tyson, and Chairman of the Council of Economic Advisors Dr. Joseph Stiglitz," March 8, 1996. The *New York Times* series "The Downsizing of America" appeared from March 3 through 9, 1996. It has been reprinted in a book incorporating additional material [*The Downsizing of America* (New York: Times Books, 1996)].

60. "Remarks by the President on Economic News and Fast Track Authority," White House Press Release, November 7, 1997 (http://www.whitehouse.gov).

61. "Press Briefing by Robert Rubin et al."

62. Judith H. Dobrzynski, "The New Jobs: A Growing Number Are Good Ones," *New York Times,* July 21, 1996, sec. 3, 1.

63. Jeff Faux, "The 'American Model' Exposed," *The Nation,* October 27, 1997, 18.

64. See, for example, Stephen S. Roach, "Stop Inflation Before It Starts," *New York Times,* June 21, 1996, A27.

65. "Press Briefing by Robert Rubin et al."

66. Alex Markels, "Restructuring Alters Middle Manager Role, but Leaves It Robust," *Wall Street Journal,* September 25, 1995, A1.

67. AMA Research, *1996 Survey on Downsizing,* 5.

68. American Management Association, "1996 AMA Survey: Summary of Key Findings," 7.

69. Markels, "Restructuring Alters Middle Manager Role," A12.

70. Ibid., A1.

71. Ibid., A12.

72. David M. Gordon, *Fat and Mean: The Corporate Squeeze of Working Americans and the Myth of Managerial "Downsizing"* (New York: The Free Press, 1996).

73. Lohr, "Though Upbeat on the Economy," 22.

2. Job Security Giving Way to Employability?

1. Charles Heckscher, *White-Collar Blues; Management Loyalties in an Age of Corporate Restructuring* (New York: Basic Books, 1995), 145 (emphasis added).

2. Ibid., 151 (emphasis added).

3. Rosabeth Moss Kanter, *World Class: Thriving Locally in the Global Economy* (New York: Simon & Schuster, 1995), 157.

4. Ibid., 22.

5. Ibid., 23.

6. Jeremy Rifkin, *The End of Work: The Decline of the Global Labor Force and the Dawn of the Post-Market Era* (New York: G. P. Putnam's Sons, 1995), xvii.

7. Norman Matloff, "Now Hiring! If You're Young," *New York Times,* January 26, 1998, A19.

8. Eileen Appelbaum, "New Technology and Work Organisation: The Role of Gender Relations," in *Pink Collar Blues: Work, Gender, and Technology,* ed. Belinda Probert and Bruce W. Wilson (Melbourne: Melbourne University Press, 1993), 68.

9. Ibid., 81.

10. Kanter, *World Class,* 155.

11. Daniel Quinn Mills, "The Changing Social Contract in American Business," *European Management Journal* 14 (October 1996): 454.

12. Lester C. Thurow, *The Future of Capitalism: How Today's Economic Forces Shape Tomorrow's World* (New York: Morrow, 1996), 308.

13. Appelbaum, "New Technology and Work Organisation," 62.

14. Kanter, *World Class,* 146.

15. Robert H. Frank and Philip J. Cook, *The Winner-Take-All Society* (New York: The Free Press, 1995), 28.

16. Ibid., 85.

17. Mills, "Changing Social Contract," 455.

18. Jeffrey Pfeffer, "Competitive Advantage through People," *California Management Review* 36 (winter 1994): 22.

19. Thurow, *The Future of Capitalism,* 16.

20. Robert Boyer, "The Economics of Job Protection and Emerging New Capital-Labor Relations," in *Employment Security and Labor Market Behavior,* ed. Christoph F. Buechtemann (Ithaca, N.Y.: ILR Press, 1993), 69–125.

21. Kanter, *World Class,* 157.

22. Richard W. Stevenson, "Bobbing and Weaving on Issue of Layoffs," *New York Times,* May 18, 1996, 31.

23. Werner Sengenberger, "Revisiting the Legal and Institutional Framework for Employment Security: An International Comparative Perspective," in *Employment Security and Labor Market Flexibility,* ed. Koshiro, 157–59.

24. Robert Pear, "High Rates Hobble Law to Guarantee Health Insurance," *New York Times,* March 17, 1998, A1.

25. Sengenberger, "Revisiting the Legal and Institutional Framework," 157.

26. Ibid., 158.

27. Robert B. Reich, "When Naptime Is Over," *New York Times Magazine,* January 25, 1998, 34.

28. Paul H. Loseby, *Employment Security: Balancing Human and Economic Considerations* (Westport, Conn.: Quorum Books, 1992), 92.

3. THE GROWTH OF CONTINGENT WORK

1. Robert Kuttner, "UPS: Off the Low Road," *Washington Post,* August 8, 1997, A21 (emphasis added).

2. The language of core and peripheral workers is reminiscent of the dual labor market discussion in labor economics circles in the 1960s and 1970s. Social ethicists such as myself need to learn from economists how a core of jobs that have the most desirable characteristics is being reconfigured. What are the similarities and differences between the primary labor market of the 1970s and the core workforce of the 1990s? For example, is the privileged core shrinking? It is also important for ethicists to remember that the image of dual and sometimes triple labor markets was used by some economists to help understand why African Americans have made limited economic progress in the United States. It also helped explain wage discrimination suffered by women workers. We need to continue to pay careful attention to how gender and race or ethnicity patterns take form in the larger picture of core and peripheral workers.

3. Just such human resource strategies have long been a key factor that allowed large Japanese corporations to guarantee long-term employment to their core male workforce.

4. Robert E. Parker, *Flesh Peddlers and Warm Bodies: The Temporary Help Industry and Its Workers* (New Brunswick, N.J.: Rutgers University Press, 1994), 144.

5. I have used data from the 1995 survey because, as the first study, it has been extensively discussed in the literature. There is preliminary information

available about the second, 1997, study. As one would expect, there was a slight decline in the percentage of the workforce who met the definition of a contingent worker in February 1997. This is a predictable finding, since the labor market was very tight in 1997. Workers who wanted standard jobs had a greater opportunity to find one in 1997. Most of the findings of the 1997 survey were consistent with the results of the 1995 survey. See "Contingent and Alternative Employment Arrangements, February, 1997," USDL 97-422, December 2, 1997.

6. U.S. Department of Labor, Bureau of Labor Statistics, "New Data on Contingent and Alternative Employment Examined by BLS," August 1995, USDL 95-318.

7. Anne E. Polivka and Thomas Nardone, "On the Definition of 'Contingent Work,'" *Monthly Labor Review* 112 (December 1989): 10.

8. U.S. Department of Labor, Bureau of Labor Statistics, "New Data on Contingent and Alternative Employment."

9. Sharon R. Cohany, "Workers in Alternative Employment Arrangements," *Monthly Labor Review* 119 (October 1996): 31.

10. Richard Belous, "How Human Resource Systems Adjust to the Shift toward Contingent Workers," *Monthly Labor Review* 112 (March 1989), 11.

11. Polivka and Nardone make a similar challenge to Belous's inclusion of all business services employees in his estimates. They are more sanguine than I am about the long-term employment prospects of employees of private security firms. See Polivka and Nardone, "Definition of Contingent Work," page 10 and page 15, note 27.

12. Gordon, *Fat and Mean,* 226–27.

13. U.S. Department of Labor, Bureau of Labor Statistics, "A Different Look at Part-Time Employment," Issues in Labor Statistics Series, Summary 96-9, April 1996, 1.

14. Chris Tilly, *Half a Job: Bad and Good Part-Time Jobs in a Changing Labor Market* (Philadelphia: Temple University Press, 1996), 1.

15. Tom Larson and Paul M. Ong, "Imbalance in Part-Time Employment," *Journal of Economic Issues* 28 (March 1994): 191.

16. Sar Levitan and Elizabeth Conway, "Part-Timers: Living on Half Rations," in *Working Part-Time: Risks and Opportunities,* ed. Barbara Warme et al. (New York: Praeger, 1992), 48.

17. Tilly, *Half a Job,* 3.

18. Kuttner, "UPS: Off the Low Road," A21.

19. Thomas Nardone, "Part-Time Employment: Reasons, Demographics, and Trends," *Journal of Labor Research* 16 (summer 1995): 291.

20. Ibid., 284.

21. Tilly, *Half a Job,* 17.

22. Nardone separated his data into the categories of women/men and minorities. Of course, some women are also minorities but, unfortunately, this article does not examine the representation of minority women among voluntary and involuntary part-time workers. Nardone, "Part-Time Employment," 278.

23. Levitan and Conway, "Part-Timers," 51.

24. U.S. Department of Labor, Bureau of Labor Statistics. "Women in the Workforce: An Overview," Report 892, July 1995, 17.

25. Nardone, "Part-Time Employment," 283.

26. Tilly, *Half a Job,* 9

27. Ibid., 52.

28. Chris Tilly, "Two Faces of Part-Time Work: Good and Bad Part-Time Jobs in U.S. Service Industries," in *Working Part-Time*, ed. Warme et al., 235.

29. Ellen Neuborne, "Temp Agencies Move Right In to Companies," *USA Today*, March 17, 1997, B1.

30. Parker, *Flesh Peddlers and Warm Bodies*, 26.

31. Kevin Henson, *Just a Temp* (Philadelphia: Temple University Press, 1996), 3.

32. Ibid.

33. This point is made about temporary jobs as a growing portion of all jobs in Sweden by Andrew Martin, "The Swedish Model: Demise or Reconfiguration?" in *Employment Relations in a Changing World Economy*, ed. Richard Locke, Thomas Kochan, and Michael Piore (Cambridge: MIT Press, 1995), 288.

34. Tilly, *Half a Job*, 155.

35. Polly Callaghan and Heidi Hartmann, *Contingent Work: A Chart Book on Part-Time and Temporary Employment* (Washington, D.C.: Economic Policy Institute, 1991), 28.

36. Cohany, "Workers in Alternative Employment Arrangements," 39.

37. Callaghan and Hartmann, *Contingent Work*, 28.

38. Sana Siwolop, "Renting the Workers, but Buying the Stock," *New York Times*, December 15, 1996, sec. 3, p. 6.

39. Parker, *Flesh Peddlers and Warm Bodies*, 29. See also Kanter, *World Class*, 151.

40. Callaghan and Hartmann, *Contingent Work*, 8.

41. Françoise J. Carré, "Temporary Employment in the Eighties," in *New Policies for the Part-Time and Contingent Workforce*, ed. Virginia L. du Rivage (Armonk, N.Y.: M. E. Sharpe, 1992), 46.

42. John Sweeney and Karen Nussbaum, *Solutions for the New Work Force: Policies for a New Social Contract* (Cabin John, Md.: Seven Locks Press, 1989), 70.

43. Anne E. Polivka, "Into Contingent and Alternative Employment: By Choice?" *Monthly Labor Review* 119 (October 1996): 56–57.

44. AMA Research, *1996 Survey on Downsizing*, 7.

45. Louis Uchitelle, "More Downsized Workers Are Returning as Rentals," *New York Times*, December 8, 1996, A1. The government survey upon which Uchitelle based his story did not include self-employed persons. It is likely that among the self-employed there are also people who are providing services on a contract basis to corporations for which they previously worked as employees.

46. Farber, *Changing Face of Job Loss*, 25.

47. Ibid., 28.

48. Richard Locke and Thomas Kochan, "Conclusions: The Transformation of Industrial Relations? A Cross-National Review of the Evidence," in *Employment Relations in a Changing World Economy*, ed. Richard Locke, Thomas Kochan, and Michael Piore (Cambridge: MIT Press, 1995), 362.

49. Guy Standing, "Global Feminization through Flexible Labor," *World Development* (Oxford, England) 17 (July 1989): 1079.

50. Carré, "Temporary Employment in the Eighties," 64.

51. Callaghan and Hartmann, *Contingent Work*, 11.

52. Parker, *Flesh Peddlers and Warm Bodies*, 98.

53. Carré, "Temporary Employment in the Eighties," 52.

54. Ibid., 56.

55. Polivka and Nardone, "On the Definition of 'Contingent Work,'" 11.

56. Carré, "Temporary Employment in the Eighties," 57.

57. Henson, *Just a Temp,* 6; Carre, "Temporary Employment in the Eighties," 57.

58. Carré, "Temporary Employment in the Eighties," 78–79. However, this example is complicated because retired employees who worked a longer period would also begin to lose social security benefits as their annual earnings exceeded the amount allowed by social security without loss of social security benefits. It is difficult to know whether retirees who worked as temps quit so that they would not lose social security benefits or were let go so that the company would not incur greater pension costs.

59. Levitan and Conway, "Part-Timers," 52.

60. Gordon, *Fat and Mean,* 224.

61. Rebecca Blank, "Are Part-Time Jobs Bad Jobs?" in *A Future of Lousy Jobs? The Changing Structure of U.S. Wages,* ed. Gary Burtless (Washington, D.C.: Brookings Institution, 1990), 133.

62. Tilly, "Two Faces of Part-Time Work," 229.

63. Blank, "Are Part-Time Jobs Bad Jobs?" 129.

64. Tilly, *Half a Job,* 4.

65. Ibid., 5.

66. Ibid., 56.

67. Ibid., 56; Levitan and Conway, "Part-Timers," 53.

68. Sweeney and Nussbaum, *Solutions for the New Work Force,* 59.

69. Blank, "Are Part-Time Jobs Bad Jobs?" 150.

70. Miriam Henry and Suzanne Franzway, "Gender, Unions, and the New Workplace: Realising the Promise?" in *Pink Collar Blues,* ed. Probert and Wilson, 133.

71. Henson, *Just a Temp,* 8.

72. "Shattering the Pension Glass Ceiling," address by Robert B. Reich to Annual Conference of Business and Professional Women USA, July 30, 1996 (http://gatekeeper.dol.gov/dol/_sec/public/media/speeches/wombiz.htm).

73. Henson, *Just a Temp,* 9.

74. Callaghan and Hartmann, *Contingent Work,* 19–21.

75. The obvious exception would be students in high school, college, or graduate school who take part-time positions precisely because the limited work hours allow them to earn some money while pursuing their education.

76. Callaghan and Hartmann, *Contingent Work,* 29.

77. Belous, "How Human Resource Systems Adjust," 9.

78. Karen Davies and Johanna Esseveld, "Factory Women, Redundancy, and the Search for Work: Toward a Reconceptualisation of Employment and Unemployment," *Sociological Review* 37 (May 1989): 220.

79. Lena Gonas, "Labor Market Adjustments to Structural Change in Sweden," in *Labor Market Adjustments to Structural Change and Technological Progress,* ed. Eileen Appelbaum and Ronald Schettkat (New York: Praeger, 1990), 180.

80. Polivka, "Into Contingent and Alternative Employment," 58.

81. Ibid.

82. Ibid.

83. Carré, "Temporary Employment in the Eighties," 49.

84. Guy Standing, "Labor Regulation in an Era of Fragmented Flexibility," in *Employment Security and Labor Market Behavior,* ed. Buechtemann, 434.

85. Tilly, *Half a Job,* 72.

86. Ibid., 152.

87. Ibid., 145.

88. Uchitelle, "Six Years in the Plus Column," D4.

89. Chris Tilly, "Short Hours, Short Shrift: The Causes and Consequences of Part-Time Employment," in *New Policies for the Part-Time and Contingent Workforce,* ed. du Rivage, 24.

90. Callaghan and Hartmann, *Contingent Work,* 11.

91. Barbara Warme, Katherina Lundy, and Larry Lundy, "Introduction," in *Working Part-Time,* ed. Warme et al., 6–7.

92. Craig McKie, "Part-Time Work in the North Atlantic Triangle: The United States, the United Kingdom, and Canada," in *Working Part-Time,* ed. Warme et al., 34.

93. Lonnie Golden, "Comment on T. Larson and P. Ong, 'Imbalance in Part-Time Employment,'" *Journal of Economic Issues* 29 (December 1995): 1199.

94. Steven Greenhouse, "High Stakes for 2 Titans: Resurgent Labor Takes on 'New Economy' in Fight over Part-time Workers at UPS," *New York Times,* August 5, 1997, A1.

95. Virginia du Rivage, "New Policies for the Part-Time and Contingent Workforce," in *New Policies for the Part-Time and Contingent Workforce,* ed. du Rivage (Armonk, N.Y.: M. E. Sharpe, 1992), 118.

96. Parker, *Flesh Peddlers and Warm Bodies,* 108 (emphasis added).

97. Ibid., 148.

98. Guy Standing, "Alternative Routes to Labor Flexibility," in *Pathways to Industrialization and Regional Development,* ed. Michael Storper and Allen Scott (London: Routledge, 1992), 273.

99. Tilly, *Half a Job,* 179.

100. Chris Benner, "Computer Workers Feel the Byte: Temp Jobs in Silicon Valley," *Dollars and Sense,* no. 207 (Sept./Oct. 1996): 25.

101. Belous, "How Human Resource Systems Adjust," 7.

102. Ibid., 8.

103. Parker, *Flesh Peddlers and Warm Bodies,* 54.

104. Tilly, *Half a Job,* 160.

4. ECONOMIC INEQUALITIES AND FEMINIST SOLIDARITY

1. Natalie J. Sokoloff, *Black Women and White Women in the Professions* (New York: Routledge, 1992), 80.

2. Barbara Reskin and Patricia Roos, *Job Queues, Gender Queues: Explaining Women's Inroads into Male Occupations* (Philadelphia: Temple University Press, 1990), 72.

3. U.S. Department of Labor, Bureau of Labor Statistics, "Women in the Workforce: An Overview," Report no. 892, July 1995, 7.

4. U.S. Department of Labor, Women's Bureau, "Facts on Working Women: Women in Management," November 1996.

5. Michael D. Yates, *Longer Hours, Fewer Jobs: Employment and Unemployment in the United States* (New York: Monthly Review Press, 1994), 27.

6. Thurow, *The Future of Capitalism,* 24.

7. *Economic Report of the President Transmitted to the Congress, 1997* (Washington, D.C.: U.S. Government Printing Office, 1997), 170.

8. "The State of Working America, 1996–97: Executive Summary" (Washington, D.C.: Economic Policy Institute, 1996) (http://www.epn.org/epi/epswa-ex.html).

9. Richard Freeman and Lawrence Katz, "Rising Wage Inequality: The United States vs. Other Advanced Countries," in *Working under Different Rules,* ed. Richard Freeman (New York: Russell Sage Foundation, 1994), 32.

10. Paul Ryscavage, "Gender-Related Shifts in the Distribution of Wages," *Monthly Labor Review* 117 (July 1994): 9.

11. U.S. Department of Labor, Bureau of Labor Statistics, "Women in the Workforce," 14.

12. John DiNardo, Nicole Forten, and Thomas Lemieux, "Labor Market Institutions and the Distribution of Wages, 1973–1992" (unpublished paper), quoted in Gordon, *Fat and Mean,* 218.

13. "The State of Working America, 1996–97: Executive Summary."

14. Deborah Anderson and David Shapiro, "Racial Differences in Access to High-Paying Jobs and the Wage Gap between Black and White Women," *Industrial and Labor Relations Review* 49 (January 1996): 280.

15. Marilyn Power and Sam Rosenberg, "Black Female Clerical Workers: Movement toward Equality with White Women?" *Industrial Relations* 32 (spring 1993): 224.

16. U.S. Department of Labor, Women's Bureau, "Facts on Working Women: Black Women in the Labor Force," no. 97-1, March 1997.

17. Power and Rosenberg, "Black Female Clerical Workers," 228, 230. During the same period, 34.3 percent of white women who had remained in the clerical category had experienced downward mobility within the clerical ranks.

18. U.S. Department of Labor, Women's Bureau. *1993 Handbook on Women Workers: Trends and Issues,* 5.

19. Cydney Pullman and Sharon Szymanski, "The Impact of Office Technology on Clerical Worker Skills in the Banking, Insurance, and Legal Industries in New York City: Implications for Training," in *Women, Work, and Computerization: Forming New Alliances,* ed. Kea Tijdens et al. (Amsterdam: North-Holland, 1989), 227.

20. Power and Rosenberg, "Black Female Clerical Workers," 230.

21. Anderson and Shapiro, "Racial Differences in Access to High-Paying Jobs," 282.

22. U.S. Department of Labor, Women's Bureau, "Facts on Working Women: Black Women in the Labor Force," no. 97-1, March 1997.

23. Sokoloff, *Black Women and White Women in the Professions,* 51–52.

24. William J. Carrington, Kristin McCue, and Brooks Pierce, "Black/White Wage Convergence: The Role of Public Sector Wages and Employment," *Industrial and Labor Relations Review* 49 (April 1996): 462–63.

25. Rita Mae Kelly, *The Gendered Economy: Work, Careers, and Success* (Newbury Park, Calif.: Sage Publications, 1991), 18.

26. U.S. Department of Labor, Women's Bureau, "Facts on Working Women: Women in Management," November 1996, table 3.

27. U.S. Department of Labor, Women's Bureau, "Facts on Working Women: Women in Management," November 1996 (http://www.dol.gov/dol/wb/public/wb-pubs/wmgt.htm).

28. Francine Blau and Lawrence Kahn, "The Gender Earnings Gap: Learning from International Comparisons," *American Economic Review* 80 (May 1992): 538.

29. U.S. Department of Labor, Women's Bureau, *1993 Handbook on Women Workers*, 29.

30. "Wage Gap Narrows—Not There Yet Though," *San Francisco Chronicle,* January 18, 1996, A20.

31. Institute for Women's Policy Research, "The Wage Gap: Women's and Men's Earnings" (http://www.iwpr.org/WAGEGAP.htm). A similar estimate showing that the gap between women's wages and men's wages is closing primarily because men's wages have declined is found in David Gordon, *Fat and Mean*, 24.

32. U.S. Department of Labor, Women's Bureau. *1993 Handbook on Women Workers,* 36.

33. Gordon, *Fat and Mean*, 179, table 7.1.

34. Chinhui Juhn, Kevin M. Murphy, and Brooks Pierce, "Wage Inequality and the Rise in Returns to Skill," *Journal of Political Economy* 101 (1993): 411.

35. Ibid., 421.

36. Gordon, *Fat and Mean*, 211–23. The same factors are considered more briefly in Lawrence Mishel and Gary Burtless, "Recent Wage Trends: The Implications for Low Wage Workers" (Washington, D.C.: Economic Policy Institute, 1995) (http://epn.org/epi/epwage.html).

37. Mishel and Burtless, "Recent Wage Trends."

38. Juhn, Murphy, and Pierce, "Wage Inequality and the Rise in Returns to Skill," 437.

39. Marcia J. Van Wagner, "Are Men's Jobs Becoming Women's Jobs? Substitution and Segmentation in the U.S. Labor Force," *Review of Radical Political Economics* 25 (September 1993): 78.

40. Barbara Baran, "The New Economy: Female Labor and the Office of the Future," in *Women, Class, and the Feminist Imagination: A Socialist-Feminist Reader,* ed. Karen V. Hansen and Ilene J. Philipson (Philadelphia: Temple University Press, 1990), 528.

41. Women's Bureau, "Earnings Differences between Women and Men."

42. Mishel and Burtless, "Recent Wage Trends."

43. Ibid.

44. Louis Uchitelle, "Raises Arrive at Bottom Rung of Labor Force," *New York Times,* May 25, 1997, D1.

45. Ibid., D6.

46. Carrie Chapman Catt, "Mrs. Catt's International Address" (Warren, Ohio: National Woman Suffrage Association, n.d.), 8.

47. One among many examples of such criticism was bell hooks, *Feminist Theory from Margin to Center* (Boston: South End Press, 1984).

48. For a discussion of some of these criticisms of the woman suffrage movement, see my *Daughters of Jefferson, Daughters of Bootblacks: Racism and American Feminism* (Macon, Ga.: Mercer University Press, 1986).

49. Sarah Lucia Hoagland, *Lesbian Ethics: Toward New Value* (Palo Alto, Calif.: Institute of Lesbian Studies, 1988).

50. Merlyn E. Mowrey, "Feminist Ethics and the 'Postmodernist Debates,'" *Annual of the Society of Christian Ethics: 1994,* 281.

51. Ibid., 282–83.

52. *Sollicitudo Rei Socialis (On Social Concern),* in *Catholic Social Thought: A Documentary Heritage,* ed. David J. O'Brien and Thomas A. Shannon

(Maryknoll, N.Y.: Orbis Books, 1996), par. 32. All papal encyclicals quoted here come from this book.

53. *Populorum Progressio (On the Development of Peoples)*, par. 3. A hint of this insight is found in Pius XI's comments on international capitalism in *Quadragesimo Anno (After Forty Years)* (see paragraph 109).

54. Kanter, *World Class*, 147.

55. Paul R. Krugman and Robert A. Lawrence, "Trade, Jobs, and Wages," *Scientific American* 270 (April 1994): 44–49.

56. *Populorum Progressio*, par. 17.

57. *Sollicitudo Rei Socialis*, par. 26.

58. Ibid., par. 38.

59. Ibid., par. 39. The encyclical indicates that this is a reference to Genesis 2:18–20. It is interesting that Genesis 2 describes Eve as a helper fit for Adam. The Hebrew term, here translated "helper," does have not any inherent connotation of subordination or inferiority. The term can be translated as a partner (in work). See Phyllis Trible, *God and the Rhetoric of Sexuality* (Philadelphia: Fortress Press, 1978).

60. United States Conference of Catholic Bishops, "Economic Justice for All," in *Catholic Social Thought*, ed. O'Brien and Shannon, par. 66.

61. Ibid., par. 67.

62. *Sollicitudo Rei Socialis*, par. 38.

63. Ibid., par. 40.

64. Ibid., par. 38.

65. *Populorum Progressio*, pars. 43–44.

66. Elizabeth A. Johnson, *She Who Is: The Mystery of God in Feminist Theological Discourse* (New York: Crossroad Publishing, 1993), 165.

67. Ibid., 137.

68. *Sollicitudo Rei Socialis*, par. 40.

69. Ibid., par. 39.

5. IS THE NEW JOB CONTRACT FAIR?

1. Thomas Donaldson, *The Ethics of International Business* (New York: Oxford University Press, 1989), 52–53.

2. Thomas Donaldson, *Corporations and Morality* (Englewood Cliffs, N.J.: Prentice-Hall, 1982), 45.

3. Philip Mattera, *Prosperity Lost* (Reading, Mass.: Addison-Wesley, 1990), 93 (emphasis added).

4. Donaldson, *Corporations and Morality*, 53.

5. Ibid., 49.

6. Ibid., 42.

7. Thomas W. Dunfee, "Business Ethics and Extant Social Contracts," *Business Ethics Quarterly* 1 (January 1991): 23–49. In a joint essay, Donaldson and Dunfee call basically the same phenomenon "real 'microsocial' contracts"; see "Toward a Unified Conception of Business Ethics: Integrative Social Contracts Theory," *Academy of Management Review* 19 (1994): 254.

8. Dunfee, "Business Ethics and Extant Social Contracts," 24.

9. Ibid., 24.

10. Donaldson and Dunfee went on to use Donaldson's concept of a "hypernorm" as a mechanism to test the binding force of extant social contracts or mi-

crosocial contracts. See, for example, "Toward a Unified Conception of Business Ethics," 265–68.

11. Donaldson and Dunfee, "Toward a Unified Conception of Business Ethics," 272.

12. Dunfee, "Business Ethics and Extant Social Contracts," 40.

13. Shari Caudron, "Will the Future Promise Job Security?" *Personnel Journal* 75 (January 1996): 48.

14. John Paul MacDuffie, "Automotive White-Collar: The Changing Status and Roles of Salaried Employees in the North American Auto Industry," in *Broken Ladders: Managerial Careers in the New Economy,* ed. Paul Osterman (New York: Oxford University Press, 1996), 96 (emphasis added).

15. Paul Osterman, "Introduction," in *Broken Ladders,* ed. Osterman, 1.

16. Sweeney and Nussbaum, *Solutions for the New Work Force,* 26.

17. United States Catholic Conference, "The Economy Pastoral Ten Years Later," *Origins: the CNS Documentary Service* 25 (November 23, 1995): 392.

18. Sheryl R. Tynes, "The Walking Wounded: Employees' Perspectives on Mergers and Acquisitions," *Sociological Inquiry* 67 (August 1997): 313.

19. Ibid., 310.

20. Ibid., 313.

21. Ibid., 306.

22. "Benefits and Job Security Are Top Workplace Concerns," *HR Focus* 69 (May 1992): 34. The actual terminology in the study was "job security." However, I believe the findings are consistent not just with job security narrowly defined, but with what I am calling employment security.

23. See, for example, "Job Security in Utility Pacts," *Monthly Labor Review* 118 (February 1995): 44–45; "Job Security for Hospital Workers," *Monthly Labor Review* 117 (December 1994): 57; "Job Security in Xerox Contract," *Monthly Labor Review* 117 (September 1994): 61; or "Job Security in Thomson Pact," *Monthly Labor Review* 117 (August 1994): 60.

24. Robb Goffee and Richard Scase, "Organizational Change and the Corporate Career: The Restructuring of Managers' Job Aspirations," *Human Relations* 45 (April 1992): 363–85; Ethel Roskies and Christiane Louis-Guerlin, "Job Insecurity in Managers: Antecedents and Consequences," *Journal of Organizational Behavior* 11 (September 1990): 345–59.

25. Paul Osterman, "Introduction," in *Broken Ladders,* 20.

26. Tynes, "The Walking Wounded," 300 (emphasis added).

27. Thurow, *The Future of Capitalism,* 27.

28. Dunfee, "Business Ethics and Extant Social Contracts," 24.

29. Donaldson and Dunfee, "Toward a Unified Conception of Business Ethics," 263.

30. Dunfee, "Business Ethics and Extant Social Contracts," 35.

31. Donaldson and Dunfee, "Toward a Unified Conception of Business Ethics," 263.

32. Michael Keeley, "Continuing the Social Contract Tradition," *Business Ethics Quarterly* 5 (April 1995): 245.

33. Thurow, *The Future of Capitalism,* 68.

34. Donaldson, *Ethics of International Business,* 88.

35. Donaldson, *Corporations and Morality,* 172.

36. Edward J. Conry, "A Critique of Social Contracts for Business," *Business Ethics Quarterly* 5 (April 1995): 200.

37. Keeley, "Continuing the Social Contract Tradition," 247.

38. Tynes, "The Walking Wounded," 304–5.

39. Michael Keeley, *A Social-Contract Theory of Organizations* (Notre Dame, Ind.: University of Notre Dame Press, 1988), 207.

40. *Laborem Exercens,* par. 12.

41. Donaldson and Dunfee, "Toward a Unified Conception of Business Ethics," 267.

42. *Rerum Novarum,* par. 34.

43. Ibid.

44. *Mater et Magistra,* par. 18.

45. *Rerum Novarum,* par. 17.

46. "Economic Justice for All," chap. 1, par. 11.

47. John Paul II, "Opening Address at the Puebla Conference," in *Puebla and Beyond: Documentation and Commentary,* ed. John Eagleson and Philip Scharper (Maryknoll, N.Y.: Orbis Books, 1980), 67.

48. One among numerous examples of this position in John Paul II's thought is *Laborem Exercens,* par. 14.

49. "Is Liberal Capitalism the Only Path?" *Origins: CNS Documentary Service* 20 (May 24, 1990): 20.

50. *Rerum Novarum,* par. 27.

51. "Economic Justice for All," par. 113.

52. *Centesimus Annus,* par. 32.

53. *Mater et Magistra,* par. 106.

54. *Centesimus Annus,* par. 32.

55. Ibid, par. 33. See also par. 34.

56. *Rerum Novarum,* par. 29.

57. Ibid., 30.

58. Ibid., 2.

59. Donal Dorr, *Option for the Poor: A Hundred Years of Vatican Social Teaching* (Maryknoll, N.Y.: Orbis Books, 1983), 257.

60. *Octogesima Adveniens,* par. 23.

61. *Laborem Exercens,* par. 8.

62. "Economic Justice for All," par. 8.

63. *Laborem Exercens,* par. 8.

64. *Centesimus Annus,* par. 57.

65. John Paul II, "Opening Address at the Puebla Conference," 60.

66. Ibid.

67. "Economic Justice for All," par. 16.

68. Ibid., par. 86.

69. *Mater et Magistra,* par. 73 (emphasis added).

70. United States Catholic Conference, "The Economy Pastoral Ten Years Later," *Origins: CNS Documentary Service* 25 (November 23, 1995): 390.

71. "Economic Justice for All," par. 185.

72. *Quadragesimo Anno,* par. 71.

73. *Gaudium et Spes,* par. 29 (emphasis added).

74. Ibid., par. 52.

75. "Letter to Women," June 29, 1995, par. 3 (http://listserv/american.edu/catholic/church/papal/jp.ii/jp.ii.html).

76. Ibid., par. 4.

77. Donaldson, *Corporations and Morality,* 53; *Ethics of International Business,* 81, 87.

78. Don Mayer and Anita Cava raise concerns about the adequacy of this theory of hypernorms to deal with gender subordination as a widespread, global phenomenon. "Social Contract Theory and Gender Discrimination," *Business Ethics Quarterly* 5 (April 1995): 257–70.

79. Nardone, "Part-Time Employment," 284 (emphasis added).

80. See also Larson and Ong, "Imbalance in Part-Time Employment," 190–91.

81. Tilly, *Half a Job,* 15.

82. "Temp" is a colloquial term for the temporary worker supplied by a temporary help agency.

83. Robert B. Reich, *The Work of Nations: Preparing Ourselves for 21st-Century Capitalism* (New York: Alfred A. Knopf, 1991).

84. Kanter, *World Class,* 23.

85. "Economic Justice for All," par. 66.

86. Donaldson, *Corporations and Morality,* 44–45.

87. Thomas W. Dunfee and Thomas Donaldson, "Contractarian Business Ethics," *Business Ethics Quarterly* 5 (April 1995): 179.

88. Donaldson, *Corporations and Morality,* 98.

89. "Human Promotion," in *The Church in the Present-Day Transformation of Latin America in the Light of the Council* (Bogota, Colombia: General Secretariate of CELAM, 1970), official English edition, ed. Louis Michael Colonnese, 58.

6. The Eucharist, Solidarity, and Justice

1. Robert Hovda, "Cultural Adaptation and the Ministry of Reconciliation," *Worship* 58 (May 1984): 252.

2. William Spohn, "Spirituality and Ethics: Exploring the Connections," *Theological Studies* 58 (March 1997): 112.

3. In this chapter, I make extensive use of the writings of Robert Hovda, particularly as found in a regular column, "The Amen Quarter," which Hovda wrote for *Worship.* Hovda was a priest, a leader in the liturgical renewal movement in the Catholic Church, an author, and an editor for the Liturgical Conference. While Hovda's field was liturgics and not ethics, he was always attentive to the moral dimension of sacramental practice. His work provides an important body of recent thought about the connection between sacraments, liturgy, and ethics.

4. Robert Hovda, "Reconciliation/Solidarity: A Hard Saying," *Worship* 62 (September 1988): 443 (emphasis added).

5. Robert Hovda, "Where Have You Been? 'Peace Liturgies' Are the Only Kind We Have!" *Worship* 57 (September 1983): 440.

6. Ibid., 439.

7. Enrique Dussel, "The Bread of the Eucharistic Celebration as a Sign of Justice in the Community," in *Can We Always Celebrate the Eucharist?* ed. Mary Collins and David Power (New York: Seabury Press, 1982), 58.

8. Ibid., 63.

9. Spohn, "Spirituality and Ethics," 115.

10. J. Bryan Hehir, "Liturgy and Social Justice: Past Relationships and Future Possibilities," in *Liturgy and Social Justice: Celebrating Rites—Proclaiming Rights,* ed. Edward M Grosz (Collegeville, Minn.: The Liturgical Press, 1989), 57.

11. Katie G. Cannon et al., *God's Fierce Whimsy: Christian Feminism and Theological Education* (New York: Pilgrim Press, 1985), 164 (emphasis added).

12. Frank Henderson, Kathleen Quinn, and Stephen Larson, *Liturgy, Justice, and the Reign of God* (Mahwah, N.J.: Paulist Press, 1989), 20.

13. Robert Hovda, "Celebrating Sacraments 'for the Life of the World,'" *Worship* 62 (January 1988): 75.

14. David Power, *The Eucharistic Mystery: Revitalizing the Tradition* (New York: Crossroad, 1993), 295–96.

15. L. William Countryman, *Dirt, Greed, and Sex: Sexual Ethics in the New Testament and Their Implications for Today* (Philadelphia: Fortress Press, 1988), 53.

16. Kathleen Corley, *Private Women, Public Meals: Social Conflict in the Synoptic Tradition* (Peabody, Mass.: Hendrickson Publishers, 1993), xv.

17. Ibid., xvii.

18. Ibid, 162.

19. Elisabeth Schüssler Fiorenza, *In Memory of Her: A Feminist Theological Reconstruction of Christian Origins* (New York: Crossroad, 1983), 119.

20. Ibid., 127–28.

21. *Populorum Progressio,* par. 47.

22. Drew Christiansen, "Notes on Moral Theology: Ecology, Justice, and Development," *Theological Studies* 51 (March 1990): 69. In this quote the North refers to the advanced industrial economies of the Northern Hemisphere and the South refers to the less economically advanced nations of the Southern Hemisphere, including the nations of sub-Saharan Africa and of Latin America.

23. Dussel, "The Bread of the Eucharistic Celebration," 62.

24. Robert Hovda, "To Recall and Renew the Ancient Memories," *Worship* 60 (May 1986): 248.

25. Robert Hovda, "Apologia for a New Column," *Worship* 57 (March 1983): 154.

26. Mary Catherine Hilkert, *Naming Grace: Preaching and the Sacramental Imagination* (New York: Continuum, 1997), 190–91.

27. Juan Luis Segundo, *The Sacraments Today,* trans. John Drury (Maryknoll, N.Y.: Orbis Books, 1974), 10.

28. Robert Hovda. "What Happened . . . ?" *Worship* 63 (January 1989): 68.

29. Margaret A. Farley, "Beyond the Formal Principle: A Reply to Ramsey and Saliers," *Journal of Religious Ethics* 7 (fall 1979): 192.

30. Ibid., 193.

31. Congregation for the Doctrine of the Faith, "Response to a 'Dubium' on Ordaining Women to the Ministerial Priesthood," *Origins* 25 (30 November 1995): 401, 403. It is especially problematic that the Congregation for the Doctrine of the Faith has promulgated a statement declaring that the policy of excluding women from the priesthood is an infallible teaching. In particular, the congregation claims that the legitimacy of this practice is one example of the infallibility of the "universal and ordinary magisterium" of the church. The term *magisterium* refers to reliable teaching authority within the church. The infallibility of the universal and ordinary magisterium hinges upon the belief that the Holy Spirit preserves the church from error in matters pertaining to the core beliefs and values of the Christian faith—beliefs and values revealed by the Deity for our salvation. One way in which the Spirit protects the core beliefs and values of the Christian faith is by assisting the church as it proclaims such truths consistently across the globe and throughout the ages. A helpful description of the ordinary, universal magisterium is found in *Lumen Gentium:*

Although the individual bishops do not enjoy the prerogative of infallibility, they can nevertheless proclaim Christ's doctrine infallibly. This is so, even when they are dispersed around the world, provided that while maintaining the bond of unity among themselves and with Peter's successor, and while teaching authentically on a matter of faith or morals, they concur in a single viewpoint as the one which must be held conclusively. ["The Dogmatic Constitution on the Church," in *The Documents of Vatican II,* ed. Walter M. Abbott (New York: America Press, 1966), par. 25.]

It remains an open question whether bishops, "dispersed around the world," are in agreement that the church has no authority to ordain women to the priesthood because the exclusion of women from the ordained ministry reflects the eternal will of God, and whether the world's bishops further teach that all members of the church are required to give assent definitively to that teaching. There was no explicit consultation with bishops throughout the world before either John Paul II's statement *Ordinatio Sacerdotalis* or the *Responsum,* which claims infallible status for the teaching that the ordained ministry ought to be reserved to men. Thus, there is no clear evidence that bishops around the world uniformly teach this position as one that must be held by all the faithful. The Congregation for the Doctrine of the Faith's position has been vigorously disputed. See, for example, "Study, Prayer Urged Regarding Women's Ordination '*Responsum,*'" Origins 27 (June 19, 1997), 75–79. See also Ladislas Orsy, "The Congregation's 'Response': Its Authority and Meaning," and Francis A. Sullivan, "Guideposts from Catholic Tradition," both in *America,* December 9, 1995, 4–6.

32. *Summa Theologica,* supplement, question 39, article 1.

33. *Ordinatio Sacerdotalis,* par. 3.

34. Cyprian Davis, *The History of Black Catholics in the United States* (New York: Crossroad, 1990), 74.

35. Jay P. Dolan, *The American Catholic Experience: A History from Colonial Times to the Present* (Garden City, N.Y.: Doubleday, 1985), 360.

36. Ibid., 365.

37. Davis, *History of Black Catholics,* 156.

38. Kenneth Himes, "Eucharist and Justice: Assessing the Legacy of Virgil Michel," *Worship* 62 (May 1988): 220.

39. Segundo, *The Sacraments Today,* 85.

40. Robert Hovda, "The Amen Corner," *Worship* 63 (September 1989): 462–63.

41. Power, *The Eucharistic Mystery,* 295.

42. Schüssler Fiorenza, *In Memory of Her,* 120.

43. Ibid., 121.

44. Dussel, "The Bread of the Eucharistic Celebration," 62.

45. Reich, *The Work of Nations,* 303.

46. "Economic Justice for All," par. 66.

47. I am using Donaldson's position only as an example, familiar to readers of chapter 5 of this book, of an argument for special concern for the socially vulnerable that is not legitimated through appeals to religious warrants. In referring to his work here, I am not suggesting that Donaldson is a person without religious commitments. Indeed, he is a Quaker.

48. Robert Hovda, *Dry Bones: Living Worship Guides to Good Liturgy* (Washington, D.C.: Liturgical Conference, 1973), 136.

INDEX

affirmative action, 55, 56, 71, 76
African Americans, 44, 51, 54–55,
133–35. *See also* blacks
age, 20, 52; old age, 20, 53, 92.
See also older men; older women;
older workers
alternative employment arrangements, 41
Appelbaum, Eileen, 30, 31
automation, 15, 69, 144 n. 29

Baran, Barbara, 76
Belous, Richard, 41, 42, 62
benefits: fringe benefits, 2, 8, 26, 37,
41, 50–54, 58, 60–62, 92, 96, 99,
101; government benefits, 3, 38;
loss of fringe benefits, 36, 42,
50–55, 58, 89, 99, 111, 141
bishops: Latin American, 108, 119;
U.S. Catholic Conference, 83–84,
94, 103–5, 108, 110–11, 118, 140;
at Vatican II, 113; and women's
ordination, 158 n. 31
blacks, 1, 4, 13, 20, 45, 64, 68–72,
77–79, 119, 134–35. *See also*
African Americans
black women, 4, 45, 55, 64, 68–72,
78–79
Blank, Rebecca, 52
Boyer, Robert, 35
Burtless, Gary, 75, 77
business services, 41, 148 n. 11

Callaghan, Polly, 47, 48, 55, 58, 59
capital, 6, 28, 32, 37, 38, 82, 93,
100, 103–5, 138; financial capital,
6, 38, 82, 100, 103; human capital, 37; intellectual capital, 28, 32
capitalism, 7, 10, 11, 36, 38, 58, 82,
85, 98, 103, 106, 130, 138; industrial capitalism, 102
caregiving, 44, 45, 53, 113–15, 132
Carré, Françoise, 48, 50, 56, 57
Catholic Church, 7, 108, 122, 125,
131–35
Catholic social thought, 6, 65, 80,
81–86, 88, 89, 93, 100–114, 116,
119, 128, 138. *See also* Roman
Catholic social thought
Centesimus Annus (John Paul II), 105
child care, 44, 113–14, 132, 135–36
Christian doctrine, 65, 86–88, 119

Christian solidarity, 85–88, 109, 119,
120–24, 128, 137, 139–42
church, 7, 85, 108, 109, 113, 120,
121–24, 128, 130–37, 142; and
racism, 133–35; as a sinful community, 130–36
class, vii–viii, 4, 57, 85, 109–11,
123; middle class, 2, 24, 105, 109,
111, 134; working class, 24, 102,
107, 136. *See also* "world class"
clerical jobs, 4, 23, 30, 47, 51, 55,
57, 58, 68–70, 116
common good, 6, 63, 82–84, 86,
105, 110, 111, 118
complementarity, 114, 132
conflict, 84, 85, 110
consent, 96–100, 112
contingent employment, viii, 6, 39,
40, 49, 91, 92, 101, 114, 124
contingent workers, viii, 2–4, 39–42,
49, 53, 55–57, 59–63, 89, 90, 111,
139, 147 n. 5
contracts. *See* employability contract;
job contract; social contract
contract workers, 2, 49–50, 55,
58–59, 62, 91, 139, 149 n. 45
Corley, Kathleen, 126, 127
corporations: loyalty of workers to,
6, 34–35, 96; responsibility to
workers, 29–32, 62–63, 138–39;
and social contract, 5–6, 90–93,
96, 98, 140
creation, doctrine of, 65, 112, 122,
132, 136, 137

Davis, Steven, 10, 11
discrimination, 55, 113, 119; age, 29;
gender, ix, 113, 115, 119, 132–33,
137; race/ethnicity, 55, 113, 115,
119, 133–35
displaced workers, 15–17, 19, 20, 29,
36–38, 49–50, 137, 141
Donaldson, Thomas, 5, 90–93, 97,
98, 101, 104, 114, 115, 118, 119,
140, 159 n. 47
downsizing, 2, 5, 9, 10, 14–15, 20,
35, 37, 49, 59, 96, 144 n. 28; of
middle management, 22; of older
workers, 5, 17
Dunfee, Thomas, 5, 90, 93, 97, 98,
101, 115, 118
Dussel, Enrique, 122, 123, 128, 129